The Intersection of Insolvency and Company Laws

PROFESSOR BOB WESSELS

Professor of International Insolvency Law, Leiden Law School

and

PAUL J. OMAR

Senior Lecturer, Sussex Law School

Editors

INSOL Europe

Nottingham • Paris

Published by
INSOL Europe
PO Box 7149
Clifton
Nottingham NG11 6WD
England

INSOL Europe website:
http://www.insol-europe.org

British Library Cataloguing in Publication Data

Library of Congress Cataloging-in-Publication Data

ISBN 978-0-9558364-2-8

Contents

Notes on Contributors

Dr. Ilona Aszódi is a Professor in the Budapest Business School in Budapest, Hungary. Email: aszodi.ilona@t-online.hu.

Dr. Alla Bobyleva is a Professor in the School of Public Administration at the MV Lomonosov Moscow State University in Moscow, Russia. Email: bobyleva@spa.msu.ru.

Dr. Norbert Csizmazia is a Lecturer in the Faculty of Law at the Eötvös Loránd University in Budapest, Hungary. Email: norbert.csizmazia@gmail.com.

Dr. Ronald Davis is an Associate Professor in the Faculty of Law at the University of British Columbia in Vancouver, Canada. Email: davis@law.ubc.ca.

Dr. Lavinia Iancu is a Lecturer in the Faculty of Law at the Tibiscus University in Timisoara, Romania. Email: office@relicons.ro.

Dr. Karin Luttikhuis is a Senior Lecturer in the Faculty of Law at the University of Tilburg in Tilburg, the Netherlands. Email: A.P.K.Luttikhuis@uvt.nl.

Dr. Tomáš Richter is a Lecturer in the Institute of Economic Studies at the Charles University in Prague, the Czech Republic. Email: tomas.richter@cliffordchance.com.

Dr. Janis Sarra is the Associate Dean and Professor in the Faculty of Law at the University of British Columbia in Vancouver, Canada as well as Director of the National Centre for Business Law. Email: sarra@law.ubc.ca.

Dr. Kathleen van der Linde is a Professor in the Faculty of Law at the University of Johannesburg in Johannesburg, South Africa. Email: kevdlinde@uj.ac.za.

Bob Wessels is the Professor of International Insolvency Law in the Leiden Law School in Leiden, The Netherlands. He is also the Distinguished Adjunct Professor of Comparative and International Insolvency Law at St. John's University School of Law, New York, United States. Email: bwessels@bobwessels.nl.

Jay L. Westbrook is the holder of the Benno C. Schmidt Chair of Business Law in the School of Law at the University of Texas in Austin, the United States. Email: jwestbrook@law.utexas.edu.

Zhang Xian-Chu is a Professor in and Associate Dean of the Faculty of Law at the University of Hong-Kong in Hong-Kong, China. Email: xczhang@hku.hk.

Editorial Preface

Insolvency is a subject that has gained considerable standing as an object of academic study and professional attention since its beginnings as an offshoot of company law or, in the case of the bankruptcy of individuals, procedural law affecting claims in relation to debt or the estates of natural persons. Insolvency may claim, like its parent subjects, to contain facets of almost every other area of the law. This may be seen because of the impact of insolvency on the organisation of commercial life, the underpinning of business relations and the fulfilment of obligations arising through contract. Also, insolvency generates penal and civil liabilities because of the mismanagement of assets and is the source of sanctions affecting the ability to conduct business. Furthermore, insolvency alters the relationship between classes of participants in business life, including the State, whose interests in maintaining economic stability are most at stake in periods of insolvency. Quite rightly, in a number of countries, insolvency is regarded as the litmus test of the country's entire civil and commercial legal system. Insolvency is, nevertheless, not just a legal discipline but also one that includes the study of economics, management and business relations and in which these interdisciplinary elements have a great role to play.

International insolvency is a more recently established branch of the study of insolvency that owes much to the phenomenon of cross-border incorporations and the conduct of business in more than one jurisdiction. It is, like insolvency, also a study of law and economic rules, to which is added the extra complication of private international law and the conflict of legal rules because of the involvement of more than one legal order. International insolvency is, however, a subject that has had more than its fair share of coverage, notably because of the insolvencies that have occurred in the international business and financial sectors. The scale and magnitude of these events have prompted the attention of commentators, drawn from both academic life and practice, resulting in a considerable number of learned publications, to which this text is designed to add.

The intention behind the present text, consisting of papers delivered at the Annual Conference of the INSOL Europe Academic Forum in Barcelona, Spain on 1–2 October 2008, is that it will form an up to date account of themes, developments and perspectives in the field of insolvency law, and particularly in relation to its comparative and international aspects. Aimed at a worldwide academic and practitioner audience, the collection of essays delivers cutting edge material, thus increasing awareness of the impact of insolvency law within domestic, regional and global contexts. This is done so as to ensure that the audience for this text receives timely notice of developments in jurisdictions representing all legal traditions and in which the improvement and reform of insolvency laws and frameworks are issues of concern to judges, practitioners and academic commentators alike. Submissions for this book have come from prominent academics and researchers in the field representing a number of jurisdictions from common law, civilian and mixed traditions. This has ensured that the contents of the research and analyses included in this text are of the highest quality and will be useful and thought-provoking. Furthermore, contributions to this text specifically address and emphasise developments in the law where the articulation of insolvency with other areas of law occurs and where insolvency is a catalyst for developments of application in general law. It is hoped that this will render the contributions here as well as the further references they contain of great value for researchers in the field.

In summary, we would like to express our appreciation to all those who have assisted in making the project a success, not least the contributors themselves, but also the administrative staff members of INSOL Europe. If not otherwise noted by the contributors, the law is stated as at 1 June 2009.

Bob Wessels
Professor of International Insolvency Law
Leiden Law School, University of Leiden
Email: bwessels@bobwessels.nl.

Paul J. Omar
of Gray's Inn, Barrister
Senior Lecturer, Sussex Law School, University of Sussex
Email: paulo@sussex.ac.uk.

A Note on the Academic Forum

The INSOL Europe Academic Forum, founded in 2004, is a constituent body of INSOL Europe, a Europe-wide association of practitioners in insolvency. The Academic Forum's primary mission is to engage in the representation of members interested in insolvency law and research, to encourage and assist in the development of research initiatives in the insolvency field and to participate in the activities organised by INSOL Europe. The membership of the Academic Forum includes insolvency academics, insolvency practitioners with recognised academic credentials as well as those engaged in the research and study of insolvency. The Academic Forum meets annually in conjunction with the main conference of INSOL Europe and also arranges half-yearly conferences around suitable themes of interest to the practice and academic communities. Previous meetings have taken place in Prague (2004), Amsterdam (2005), Monaco (2007), Leiden and Barcelona (2008) as well as Brighton (2009).

At the Monaco Conference, Professor Bob Wessels, Professor in International Insolvency Law at the University of Leiden, was elected Chair of the Management Board for a three-year term. Dr. Paul Omar, (University of Sussex, Brighton, United Kingdom) was elected to serve as Secretary to the Board, while Florian Bruder (Max Planck Institute, Hamburg, Germany) and Professor Ulrich Haas (University of Zurich, Switzerland) are ordinary members of the Board. A Supervisory Committee has also been established as a consultative board for Academic Forum projects. Its membership includes senior insolvency academics and practitioners.

With sponsorship made available by Edwin Coe LLP over a three-year period from 2007–2010, the Academic Forum has been able to offer young scholars travel grants to attend its conferences, research grants for scholarly projects as well as prizes for outstanding legal scholarship awarded on the basis of monographs and publications. Edwin Coe LLP has also kindly sponsored an annual lecture to be given by a scholar of international repute.

Enhancing existing links within the academic insolvency world, the Academic Forum is also co-operating with the INSOL International Academic Group, under the chairmanship of Professor Ian Fletcher (University College London), with view to expanding the membership base and attracting researchers and scholars to attend and deliver papers at the conferences of both organisations. This co-operation will also see reciprocal advertising of group conferences and events and the development of links through the websites of the respective groups.

The Academic Forum's next annual meeting is scheduled to take place in conjunction with the INSOL Europe conference in Stockholm on 30 September–1 October 2009, with future conferences planned for Vienna (2010) and Venice (2011). Details of academic conferences will be posted at the Academic Forum website: www.insol-europe.org/academic/ as and when available. On-line registration for the academic conferences will also feature on the website. Further information about the work of the Academic Forum can also be obtained via the Academic Forum website.

PART I
COMPARATIVE AND INTERNATIONAL INSOLVENCY LAW

Chapter 1

Crisis Management in Russian Companies

Alla Bobyleva

Introduction[1]

The legislation of countries with a developed market economy and the tradition of following ethical business norms protect the investor effectively in crises in Europe and the USA. In countries with transitional economies, and in Russia in particular, the protection of investors is not always sufficient. Let us consider the reasons which have led to this situation, and the main ways of protection and enforcement for investors. This task is especially urgent given conditions within global economic and financial crises.

One of the crucial elements of investor protection in any crisis is the guarantees protecting their interests during the transfer of property rights. The Russian regulatory framework for property redistribution procedures started to develop at the beginning of the 1990s and has not been finally formed up to the present day. During the last 10–20 years, the property redistribution procedure took place under continuously changing conditions in the legal system as well as under complex law enforcement procedures and administrative hurdles. Transaction costs for legal property transfers were high compared to the low costs of illegal takeovers. Unlike the situation in western countries, Russian stock market and corporate governance requirements had a limited influence on property redistribution.

When a transfer of capital took place, it was done mostly outside the legal field and organized markets. Taking control over the company was often carried out using either illegal methods or legal devices to the detriment of the rights and legitimate interests of some groups of investors and often with the violation of principles of business ethics. Hostile takeovers became one of the most widespread methods of gaining the control over the company.

The share of hostile mergers and acquisitions was especially high during "perestroika" and the following period. According to the author's estimations, 70-80% of acquisitions might be considered unfriendly. The peculiarities of the great number of mergers and acquisitions transactions consisted in the use of measures,

[1] The author would like to thank Edwin Coe LLP for their sponsorship of the Academic Forum, which enabled the author to benefit from a travel grant to present this paper at the Barcelona Conference.

methods and technologies which did not correspond to certain principles of business behaviour and which contradicted some market laws. Such hostile acquisitions may be characterized as unfair or incorrect, even uncivilized.

The Spread of Unfair Acquisitions

The main reason for the spread of unfair acquisitions was the fact that their cost was usually lower than the cost of the civilized market acquisition. Higher costs of the civilized acquisition are caused by the following reasons:

- The transparency of information about the possibility of mergers and acquisitions transactions is usually accompanied by an increase in the share price of the target company.
- In Russia, the corporate aggressor often does not wish to spend money on the purchase of a required shareholding in the company-target. It may achieve success by raiding methods. For instance, the practice shows that the control of shareholders over the activity of executive top-management is insignificant and the realization of ownership rights is complicated. In such circumstances, the struggle for the operating management and for the benefits which it provides, obtains special value and it is often expressed in the interception of management functions.
- Bankruptcy laws, which were often used for property repartition, contained many regulations which reduced the price of the takeover (a low threshold for liabilities, a specific procedure for the appointment and control of an administrative receiver, the opportunity for debt repayment by third parties together with the direct participants of the bankruptcy process, etc.). Besides, it did not prohibit asset stripping by means of deliberate bankruptcies.
- Aggressor companies used the so-called "administrative resource" to reduce the price of the transaction and to lobby the interests of particular business groups by corruption of authorities. For instance, the regional executive authorities conspired to form the so-called "regional economy" by taking control over basic regional enterprises. For this purpose, privatization was used as an element for reducing the price of the transaction. State-owned property became part of the share capital of business entities. In such a way, the market mechanism for transactions was broken and thus the possibility for non-transparent transactions occurred.

The most widespread unfair takeover techniques are:

- proxy fights;
- stock watering;
- bankruptcy; and
- consolidation.

In countries with a developed market economy, there are regulations that stipulate that the aggressor company must disclose its plans when purchasing a significant share holding (for instance, five percent or more). In Russia, such regulations are not yet enforced. Therefore, it is still possible for Russian enterprises to have an unfriendly shareholder controlling a sufficient number of shares to have a general meeting of shareholders summoned and to replace the top–management of the company as well as to alter the composition of the board of directors, etc. Also, there are known cases of illegal share-transfers, the creation of double registers and the loss of those registers.

From an initial perspective, stock watering and the consolidation of stock seem to be two very opposite tools. However, they are both used in unfair takeovers. Additional issue of stock in the absence of market information enables the acquisition of significant share holdings and leads to the appearance of new owners and changes in the structure of ownership. Consolidation of shares and their buyout by a small group of shareholders may lead to the same results as stock watering.

Despite the constant updating of bankruptcy laws, they still cannot fully prevent the unfair repartition of the property by means of bankruptcy. According to a number of different opinions, in recent years 20-40% of legal proceedings related to bankruptcies "by order" were brought before the courts. However, it is very difficult to prove this.

The possibility of unfair takeovers plays a negative role not only at the microeconomic level, but it also influences negatively the development of financial markets and it has serious macroeconomic consequences, including:

- A reduction of investments into the country;

- The decrease in the free floating of shares as a result of dominating shareholders' aspirations to snatch control over a maximum number of shares, to mitigate the risk of concentration of large share holdings in the market in the interests of potential aggressors (for instance, many large banks in Russia do not perform open sale of shares);

- An increase in the issuer's risk, which contributes to the underestimation of Russian corporations and prevents the growth of their capital;

- The reduction of information about the company to decrease the opportunities of the takeover thus creating an unattractive image;

- A decrease in the efficiency of the distribution of natural resources and use of national wealth; and

- A negative change in the ownership structure.

Unfair corporate takeovers may be considered as a factor which reduces the efficiency of the economic development of the country and attractiveness of the investment climate for foreign investors. Violation of investors' rights leads to the growth of risk. Hence, investment and entrepreneurial activity also reduces the efficiency of the economy as a whole.

In recent years, people have come to an understanding that preventing incorrect corporate takeovers is a necessary prerequisite for the increase in the efficiency and stability of the economic system and its attractiveness for investors. Globalization strengthens requirements for any enterprise's actions, which leads to general comprehension of certain universal principles of business behaviour.

Eliminating Unfair Acquisitions

The main measures allowing for the elimination of the possibility of unfair takeovers or at least to lower their percentage share of transactions generally are the following:

- Legal regulation;
- Enforcement;
- Control of non-governmental organizations through compliance with business standards.

First of all, let us consider the opportunities and immediate perspectives of the enhancement of legal regulation.

It is necessary to note that the Laws "On Joint-Stock Companies" (2002) and "On Insolvency (Bankruptcy)" (2002) have greatly limited the possibility of uncivilized takeovers. Nevertheless, the regulation of takeovers in the Russian legislation still contains many drawbacks. In our opinion, the primary measures that require amendment to the law are the following:

- Integration of the registrars in order to increase their independence from issuers, avoid "parallel" registers and suppress illegal transfer of shares.

- Finalization of regulations for companies regarding large purchases: presently the rules of property transfer to large companies (over 1000 shareholders) are not sufficiently detailed.

- To give the shareholders of the companies under bankruptcy proceedings the primary right to meet the requirements of their creditors. Currently, in the case of unfair takeovers, interested participants may use the procedure "of financial rehabilitation" in Articles 113 and 125 of the Law "On Insolvency (Bankruptcy)", according to which any person has the right to pay off all the company's debts on equal terms with the shareholder and thus to become the owner of the company.

- Removal of the legislation on privatization on special terms, which give the possibility of using transactions with specific non-market conditions and to leave the auction as the only possible mechanism of privatization.

- The introduction of regulations which exclude the possibility of hearings of corporate disputes by regular courts as well as expansion of the network of commercial courts. Practice shows that it is more difficult to come to an agreement with courts which specialize in the consideration of certain types of cases.

As mentioned above, the methods used for unfair takeovers are not always due to drawbacks in legislation; laws are frequently simply broken. With this regard, in our opinion, it is necessary to introduce a special agency to supervise the takeover process or to give additional powers to the Federal Service on Financial Markets. One of the possible ways for organizing similar control is to use the experience of some countries, the United Kingdom for instance, where the core participant in the reorganization procedure is the Office of Fair Trading (OFT). It is a supervising body which concentrates on the observance of the rules of fair competition.

The state system of supervision in the United Kingdom is supplemented with an original non-government system: for example, the Panel on Takeovers and Mergers has existed since 1968. It has developed rulings on self-regulation, in particular the City Code on Takeovers and Mergers and rules governing the substantial acquisition of shares. It is necessary to note that non-government organizations work out business standards, not laws. This experience may be very important for Russia. Due to the short-term period of the country's development outside the previous framework of a command economy, the corporate culture has not yet been formed and business ethical standards have not been developed. The first step in this direction was the working out of recommended norms in the Russian Code of Corporate Behaviour which was approved by the Government of the Russian Federation and recommended by the Federal Commission on Securities in 2002.

Gradually the participants of the business processes should come to an understanding that public reputation is more valuable, while usage of criminal or semi-criminal ("grey") methods of mergers and acquisitions is not profitable. Therefore, one of the objectives both of state authorities and non-governmental supervising organizations is to spread information regarding best practices and to warn about unfair transactions.

In general, our legislation on the enforcement and control of NGOs should create conditions in which the civilized transfer of property rights might cost less in comparison to unfair transactions. The government strategy should be aimed at using a liberal market approach. It should concentrate not on the liquidation of the phenomenon as such, but on the gradual elimination of the reasons for the phenomenon by means of deep changes in the economy, in standards of business behaviour and through regulatory enactments.

Besides the presence of unsolved problems of investor protection in cases of mergers and acquisitions, there are some other problems with which foreign investor can come into collision in Russia:

- The processes of valuation, transfer of business or settlement of disputes are not well organized in certain regions.

- Sometimes, potential investors can receive the suggestion to buy business which is located on leased lands: a lot of businesses in Russia are located on lands that are public equity and can be only leased for 49 or 99 years. In these cases, the risks of changing conditions (the volatility of leasing fees, property transfers, etc.) must be taken into account by investors.

- It is well known that small and middle businesses are more profitable, their pay-back period is lower, they are more appropriate in a crisis as a whole. But informed investors are aware of the fact that investment partnerships in Russia have much more probability to be successful if it is initiated by government or at least supported by government. But government almost always initiates and gives guarantees for large projects! There are a lot of formal words for supporting small business in Russia but only a few steps are taken in this direction.

- The value of intangible assets is very low in Russia, especially in small businesses. For example small shops, bars, restaurants can have their own mini-brands in regions but in practice they do not have any value in case of transfer of ownership. Foreign investor should take it into account when considering the exit terms.

- Business is often sold at a much higher price than in official documents, i.e. some "grey schemes" are used. In these cases the investor can waste part of his money in secondary sales.

- Sometimes business in Russia seems to be undervalued and the purchase looks very profitable. But in practice such purchases can be rather risky. A good example of it is the situation with Renault which became the strategic investor in the Russian Automobile giant "AvtoVAZ". In addition to a crisis in operations and finance, Renault came face-to-face with "grey" schemes, a criminal economy and cash from "hand-to-hand" schemes, etc.

- It is also necessary for potential investors to check compliance with ecological, health and other similar standards. The former owner could have some informal agreements with authorities concerning the realization of standards but the new owner may pay a lot of money to meet the standards.

Conclusion

The character of the development of investment partnerships, which have been not sufficiently fast, is often explained by the difference between the views of Russian and foreign investors on the necessary amount of reinvestment, the need for transparency and the conduct of IPOs. Additional risks related to the short period of the functioning of the market economy and insufficient experience of Russian partners influence the establishment of foreign investors in Russia.

However, one can observe the problem of investment partnership development from a different angle. No doubt, the reliable protection of creditors is the compulsory component of attractive investment climate, but low risks are as a rule accompanied by the low income. Russia is the country in which the foreign investor has been receiving high profits for the last 20 years. The fact that Russian legislation at the moment complies with international requirements lowers the risks for investors and in the near future one can expect the inflow of foreign capital to Russia as to the region with relatively high profitability, which will enable to overcome the world financial crisis faster.

As additional risks decrease, one can recommend foreign investors to disseminate the principles of civil society through investment partnership agreements – it is necessary to indicate the type of "marital agreement": exit conditions and methods for dispute-resolution.

Chapter 2

Deficiencies in the Hungarian Insolvency Act and Possible Remedies

Norbert Csizmazia

Introduction*

The Hungarian Insolvency Act was adopted in 1991.[1] It has been amended several times since its adoption, but its most serious flaws remain unfixed. Most notably, there is no corporate rescue procedure (other than a composition proceeding existing only in the statute book), there is no procedure offering a fresh start for over-indebted individuals and there are no private international law rules for non-European Union insolvencies.

In 2003, a Committee was appointed to prepare and draft a new Insolvency Act. The Committee prepared a concept paper that contained the guidelines of a new insolvency act, although these guidelines were too rudimentary to form the basis of legislation. The concept paper did not envisage creating an insolvency procedure for individuals, but proposed a new framework for corporate insolvency: an insolvency proceeding with a single entry point leading to either reorganization or liquidation after the creditors' meeting. However, in late 2004, the Committee was dissolved before it could have produced draft legislation.[2]

The Ministry of Justice, responsible for drafting insolvency legislation since 2005,[3] has failed to implement a comprehensive reform of insolvency law ever since. A government decision on the guidelines of a new insolvency act was

---

* The author is indebted to Judge Andrea Csőke (Metropolitan Court, Budapest) for helpful suggestions and many invaluable discussions. The author would also like to thank Edwin Coe LLP for their sponsorship of the Academic Forum, which enabled the author to benefit from a travel grant to present this paper at the Barcelona Conference.

[1] Act XLIX of 1991. The Act came into effect on 1 January 1992.

[2] The dissolution of the Committee was a consequence of the dismissal of the Secretary of State under whose supervision the Committee was working.

[3] Until 2004, the Ministry of Finance was responsible for preparing legislation in the area of insolvency law. In 2004 the Committee for the Re-codification of Insolvency Law (under the auspices of the Prime Minister's Office) played an important role in the Insolvency Act. After the dissolution of this Committee in late 2004, the responsibility for preparing insolvency legislation was transferred to the Ministry of Justice.

adopted in early 2005,[4] but only piecemeal reforms followed. This is in sharp contrast to the attention paid to insolvency law by legislators all over the world and also to the Hungarian government's activity in the field of company law, where the third new Companies Act has been introduced since the transition.[5]

This paper is limited to corporate insolvency law. This limitation flows from the fact that the Hungarian Insolvency Act ("IA") only applies to corporate debtors and does not cover individuals and unincorporated businesses (sole traders). It will also give an overview of the IA with special emphasis on the most recent amendments and identify the most important deficiencies of the legislation. Finally, it will examine the position of insolvency law in the curriculum of Hungarian law faculties and the state of insolvency law scholarship in Hungary, asserting that the low standing of insolvency law as an academic discipline in Hungary has adversely affected the quality of legislation in this field.

Overview of the Current Insolvency Act

The IA follows a two-track approach; it contains rules on two distinct procedures. The 'bankruptcy proceeding' [*csődeljárás*] is aimed – in theory at least – at the rescue of ailing, but viable companies.[6] The objective of the 'liquidation proceeding' [felszámolási eljárás] is the maximisation and realisation of the debtor's assets and finally their distribution among the creditors.

"Bankruptcy Proceedings": Lack of an Automatic Stay[7]

The "bankruptcy proceeding" is virtually non-existent. The simple reason for that is that presentation of a petition for the opening of a bankruptcy proceeding[8] does not result in an automatic stay of creditor action. Creditors, secured and unsecured alike, can enforce their claims despite the presentation of the petition. The court will make an order imposing a moratorium only if the required proportion of the creditors consents to it.

[4] Government Decision No. 1094/2005 (IX. 19.)

[5] Strictly speaking, the first Companies Act pre-dated the transition: it was enacted in 1988 (Act VI of 1988). The second Companies Act was adopted in 1997 (Act CXLIV of 1997), the third in 2006 (Act IV of 2006).

[6] "Bankruptcy proceeding" is the formal translation of the Hungarian word "csődeljárás". The current Hungarian terminology is rather unfortunate. In pre-WWII Hungarian law (Act XVII of 1881) the same Hungarian word stood for the liquidation proceeding. Interestingly, the new meaning of the word never received recognition in everyday usage and the word is still frequently used (e.g. in newspapers) to refer to liquidation.

[7] For a more detailed account of the problems with the "bankruptcy proceeding" see A. Csőke, "Hungary: Pitfalls of the Current Legislation and Potential for Future Reforms", in K. Gromek Broc and R. Parry (eds), Corporate Rescue – An Overview of Recent Developments, 2nd edition, Kluwer 2006, 215-239.

[8] A petition for the opening of a bankruptcy proceeding can only be presented by the debtor. More precisely, by the debtor's directors with the prior approval of the shareholders. No substantive standard of insolvency needs to be satisfied.

To that end, the debtor has to convene a meeting of the creditors within 30 days of the presentation of the petition and obtain the consent of more than 50 per cent of the creditors holding a matured claim and more than 25 per cent of those holding an non-matured claim and in addition the consenting creditors must represent together at least two-thirds in value of all the claims.[9] If the required majority is obtained, the court makes an order for a moratorium of 60 (or 120) days, during which the debtor – supervised by a court-appointed administrator – tries to reach a composition with the creditors. The composition needs to be approved by the administrator and finally sanctioned by the court, by which the proceeding is concluded.

In practice, however, petitions for the opening of bankruptcy proceedings are rarely presented (20 applications in 2007, 15 in 2008) and creditors almost never give their consent to a moratorium (1 court order in 2007, none in 2008). The petition for a bankruptcy proceeding only accelerates creditor action and leads to the dissipation of the remaining assets of the company.

Liquidation Proceedings: Commencement Criteria

By contrast, the number of liquidation proceedings is steadily on the rise.[10] A liquidation proceeding can be opened by the court either upon the application of the debtor or the application of a creditor. Since 1 September 2007, the debtor may make an application simply by declaring its state of insolvency or imminent insolvency, without having to satisfy any substantive standard of insolvency.[11] A creditor can apply for the opening of liquidation proceedings on one of four grounds:

- failure of the debtor to dispute or pay a contractual debt within 15 days after maturity and failure to settle the debt after a subsequent written demand of the creditor;
- failure of the debtor to pay a debt within the deadline set by a final court order;
- unsuccessful judicial enforcement (execution) of a debt; or
- failure of the debtor to respect its obligations under a "bankruptcy composition".[12]

It can be seen from the above that the IA relies on the cash flow (or commercial insolvency) test. The debtor's overall financial situation is not assessed and no general cessation of payments test is used. A creditor holding a single

[9] IA § 9(4).

[10] The number of liquidation proceedings opened in 2005: 7,957, in 2006: 9,439, in 2007: 9,572, in 2008: 11,322.

[11] IA § 22.

[12] IA § 27(2).

matured debt (with no requirement of a minimum amount) is entitled to apply for a winding up order. As a result, creditors often resort to liquidation instead of execution, in order to put pressure on debtors to pay, although small firms, e.g. trade suppliers, do not usually exploit this potential of a petition for liquidation, for fear of losing their customers.

Avoidance of Transactions

An important way of wealth maximisation is the recovery of assets by the avoidance of certain pre-petition transactions. The rules on transaction avoidance were reformed in 2004.[13]

Until 2004, liquidators usually refrained from challenging transactions, because they could commence avoidance proceedings only in their own name, at their own risk. The 2004 amendment changed this by providing that the liquidator acts in the name of the debtor and therefore the costs of the proceedings are borne by the insolvent estate. (As before the amendment, creditors are also entitled to invoke the grounds of avoidance on equal basis with the liquidator. In this case, the costs of the proceedings have to be paid out of the creditor's own funds.)

The 2004 amendment also clarified the types of vulnerable transactions. Prior to the amendment, the IA only provided for the avoidance of:
- gratuitous transactions;
- transactions at an undervalue (i.e. with a gross disproportion between the mutual performances); and
- a third class of transactions, defined as "other transactions designed to defraud creditors and resulting in a diminution of the assets of the debtor".

The uniform twilight period was 1 year from the presentation of the petition for the opening of the liquidation. In respect of the third group of transactions it was unclear whether the debtor and its counterparty had to act in bad faith when concluding the contract. Some courts required the liquidator to show a fraudulent intent on part of the parties to the challenged transaction, while other courts gave a more objective interpretation to this provision and invalidated transactions even if the counterparty was in good faith.[14]

The IA (as amended in 2004) distinguishes between three categories of vulnerable transactions with different twilight periods:
- fraudulent transactions (entered into in the 5 years prior to the petition or thereafter);
- transactions at an undervalue (entered into in the 2 years prior to the petition or thereafter); and

---

[13] Act XXVII of 2004, § 53.

[14] In 2008 the Supreme Court had to interpret this provision (in a case that had to be decided on the basis of the text as it stood before the 2004 amendment) and ruled that a transaction fell into the third group only if there was a fraudulent intent on part of both the debtor and the counterparty.

- preferential transactions (entered into in the 90 days prior to the petition or thereafter).[15]

Transactions at an undervalue include both gratuitous transactions and transactions with a gross disproportion between the mutual performances. Preferential transactions are defined as "contracts and other juridical acts the object of which is giving an advantage to one of the creditors". For this last category, the IA also gives two examples: the modification of a contract in favour of a creditor and the provision of security for a past debt.

In addition to these three classes of transactions, the IA also expressly allows for the reversal of payments and other performances, if a preference was given thereby to a creditor and the payment or other performance was outside the ordinary course of business of the debtor. Again, there is a statutory example: the settlement of a debt before its maturity. [16] This fourth category was added to cover purely factual acts that would not qualify as "contracts or other juridical acts".

However, the amendment failed to clarify the effect of a successful avoidance, which remained controversial until late 2008, when the Supreme Court eliminated this lacuna in the legislation by adopting the "uniformity decision" 3/2008 PJE.[17] In this decision the Court ruled that the successful avoidance results in the invalidity of the challenged transaction. The provisions of the Civil Code on the invalidity of contracts apply, i.e. the court will order the restoration of the position before the contract *(in integrum restitutio)*. In case of a transaction with a gross imbalance between the mutual performances, the court may instead make an order for payment of an additional sum by the counterparty to the insolvency estate to restore the balance between the performances.[18]

The Supreme Court also pointed out that a creditor who brings an action to avoid a pre-petition transaction and succeeds will not be able to retain the property returned by the counterparty, as that would be contrary to the collective nature of the liquidation proceeding and would be tantamount to an individual enforcement by the creditor. Therefore it is hard to understand why the IA gives a locus standi to the creditors.

Directors' Liability for Wrongful Trading

The directors' personal liability for wrongful trading was introduced in 2006 into Hungarian insolvency law. It applies to those who have served as directors or acted as shadow directors in the 3 years prior to the commencement of liquidation proceedings. The liability arises, if the directors have not performed their tasks in the best interests of the creditors from the time when they knew or ought to have

[15] IA § 40(1).

[16] IA § 40(2).

[17] A "uniformity decision" [jogegységi határozat] of the Supreme Court is binding on all subordinate courts.

[18] Civil Code § 237(1)-(2).

concluded that the company will be unable to pay its debts as they fall due (imminent insolvency). A defence is available, if the director shows that he took all the measures necessary to minimise the loss of creditors. There is an irrebuttable presumption of 'wrongful trading' if the director has not performed his obligation to publish annual accounts.[19]

In terms of procedure, the liability for wrongful trading can be enforced in a two-stage procedure:

- During the liquidation proceeding, the creditors or the liquidator have to apply to the court for a declaratory judgment, i.e. that the director(s) failed to act in the best interests of the creditors after the onset of imminent insolvency.
- After the conclusion of the liquidation proceeding, creditors with unsatisfied claims have 90 days to apply to the court for an order requiring the directors to satisfy these claims.

This procedure means that the director, if held liable, will not contribute to the insolvency estate and therefore the liquidator has no real interest in making applications for declaratory judgments.[20]

The funding of wrongful trading actions is also unclear. Whilst an amendment of the IA in 2004 clarified that transaction avoidance proceedings are initiated by the liquidator on behalf of the corporate debtor, i.e. the liquidator acts in the name of the debtor and thus the costs of the proceedings are borne by the insolvent estate; there is no similar provision in relation to wrongful trading actions.

Nor do the wrongful trading provisions give a clear guidance to directors as to what is expected of them. The single statutory presumption (about the director's omission to file annual accounts) can hardly be regarded as sufficient guidance. One could assume that directors, in order to avoid liability for wrongful trading, will apply for the opening of liquidations over-hastily. However, directors are not entitled to apply for the opening of liquidation proceedings without the prior approval of shareholders. [21]

For the above reasons it is unsurprising that there has been no reported case law on the new provisions on wrongful trading in the two years since their introduction and they are likely to remain law in the books.

[19] IA § 40(1).
[20] IA § 40(2).
[21] A "uniformity

Secured Claims in Liquidation

Under Hungarian insolvency law, the liquidator has the exclusive power to realise and distribute the assets of the debtor company. Not even secured creditors are entitled to enforce their proprietary rights after the commencement of the liquidation. Instead they are entitled to payment in full out of the proceeds of sale of the encumbered assets, after the deduction of:

- the costs of the preservation and the sale of the assets; and
- a further 5 per cent of the proceeds as remuneration for the liquidator.[22]

Thus, the secured creditors are in a position similar to German secured creditors with an *Absonderungsrecht or Spanish secured creditors with a privilegio especial.*

This is subject to one exception: the holder of an enterprise charge (a distant relative of the English floating charge)[23] is only entitled to partial priority. Only 50 per cent of the proceeds of sale of the encumbered assets (minus the costs of the sale)[24] will be paid directly to the holder of the enterprise charge, the other 50 per cent is reserved for the satisfaction of preferential claims and only the surplus – if any – will be paid to the secured creditor.

This quasi full priority of secured creditors in respect of the proceeds of sale of the encumbered assets was only gradually re-introduced: In liquidation proceedings opened before 1 September 2001, an extensive list of privileged claims was granted absolute preference over secured claims. These preferential claims included not only the expenses of the proceeding and the remuneration of the liquidator, but – inter alia – also the debts due to employees, the claims of the Wage Guarantee Fund and the costs of remedying any damage caused by the debtor company to the environment.

It was in the context of the second post-transition reform of secured transactions law (adopted in 2000, in force since 2001)[25] that an amendment of the IA introduced the partial priority of secured creditors was introduced: 50 per cent of the proceeds of the sale of the encumbered asset – minus the costs of the sale – had to be paid directly to the secured creditor, the other 50 per cent was reserved for the preferential claims and only the surplus – if any – could be paid to the secured creditor. This limited priority was restricted to the holders of charges created earlier than one year before the commencement of the liquidation.

---

[22] IA § 49/D (1).

[23] For a comparison of the Hungarian enterprise charge and the English floating charge see N. Csizmazia, "Reform of the Hungarian Law of Security Rights in Movable Property" (2008) 1 Juridica International 181, 185-186.

[24] Strangely, IA § 49/D (2) refers only to the deduction of the costs of the sale, but not to the deduction of the costs of preservation or the 5 per cent of the proceeds as remuneration of the liquidator.

[24] Act CXXXVII of 2000.

Finally, a further amendment (adopted in 2006, in force since 1 January 2007) [26] granted absolute priority to secured creditors, provided that the charge was created before the commencement of the liquidation proceeding. Thus the rule, that excluded the holders of "late charges" (i.e. charges created within one year of the commencement of the liquidation) from the scope of the priority rule, was also abolished. As already mentioned above, the limited priority (to 50 per cent of the proceeds) was retained for enterprise charges.

The distinction made between the treatment of claims secured by "ordinary" charges and claims secured by enterprise charges had been present in the early drafts of the bill, then it was dropped, but re-introduced in the very last moment as a compromise between the two main interest groups participating in the consultations. [27] As a justification, the explanatory notes (to Act VI of 2006) expressly refer to carve-out techniques adopted in other European jurisdictions that recognise all-assets security rights, namely the "prescribed part" (a share of the assets subject to a floating charge to be set aside for the benefit of unsecured creditors) under the English insolvency legislation [28] and the 55 per cent carve-out under Swedish legislation on *företagsinteckning.* [29]

However, this distinction is causing problems in practice as liquidators face situations where the assets of the debtor company are subject not to an enterprise charge, but to a series of "ordinary charges" granted to the same creditor which together cover substantially the whole of the enterprise. Under a formal interpretation of the law, the 50 per cent carve-out does not apply. Under a purposive interpretation focusing on the substance and the economic effect, the 50 per cent carve-out should apply. It is unlikely that Hungarian courts would follow the second interpretation, thus the 50 per cent carve-out will be easily circumvented by creditors. [30]

---

[26] Act VI of 2006.

[27] The explanatory notes expressly mention the consultation held on 2 December 2005 between representatives of the Hungarian Banking Federation, the Association of Insolvency Practititoners and the Ministry of Justice.

[28] Insolvency Act 1986, s.176A and Insolvency Act 1986 (Prescribed Part) Order 2003.

[29] In 2005, the old legislation on företagshypotek was replaced by the new law on företagsinteckning. (The Lag (2003:528) om företagsinteckning took effect on 1 January 2004, but "old floating charges" granted before 1 January 2004 could be enforced in insolvency proceedings opened before 1 January 2005.) The "old floating charge" (företagshypotek) was less universal, important classes of assets (e.g. bank deposits, shares, bonds and real property) were exempt from its coverage, but it conferred on its holder priority over the entire patrimony of the debtor company. The "new floating charge" (företagsinteckning) extends to all real and personal property of the debtor, but the priority was limited to 55 per cent of the total value of the assets. However, the 55 per cent carve-out had a rather short life. The Swedish legislator recently abolished it and from 1 January 2009 claims secured by företagsinteckning are again entitled to full priority from all the assets of the debtor company.

[30] The first drafts of the new Hungarian Civil Code (the bill of which is currently before the Parliament) proposed to abolish the enterprise charge. It was argued that there is no need for a distinct all-assets security right, since the "ordinary" registered non-possessory charge can be granted over all the movables of the debtor, who retains the right to dispose of the charged assets in the ordinary course of business. In other words, the availability of the 'floating lien' (as known under Art. 9 UCC) makes the English-style floating charge redundant. As to immovables, it was argued that creditors take separate mortgages over the immovables anyway, since charges and mortgages registered in specialist registers have priority over a floating charge, even if the latter is registered earlier. However, the final bill retains the enterprise charge as a distinct security device.

It is also remarkable that the Hungarian carve-out provision is not for the benefit of unsecured creditors. The 50 per cent of the proceeds that is not paid directly to the holder of the enterprise charge can only be used for the satisfaction of preferential claims. If anything remains after the satisfaction of these, the surplus goes to the holder of the enterprise charge and not to the unsecured creditors.[31]

Debtors with Insufficient Assets

In approximately 90 per cent of all liquidation proceedings, the debtor has no or insufficient assets to fund the administration of the liquidation proceeding.[32] These cases (thus the majority of liquidation proceedings) are conducted in a simplified way ("simplified liquidation proceedings"),[33] and the state pays for the remuneration of liquidators. State expenditures on this account totalled around € 6,500,000 between 2002 and 2006. In 2008 alone, the state paid € 1,772,220 to insolvency practitioners as remuneration for acting as liquidators in 6,525 simplified liquidation proceedings.[34]

The lack of assets to cover the costs of the proceedings leads in several jurisdictions to the closure of proceedings.[35] In 2008, an insolvency judge and some Members of the Parliament proposed to amend the IA so as to enable the court to refuse the opening of the proceedings against debtors with no assets to cover the costs of the proceeding. According to the proposal, an unsuccessful attempt by the tax authority to enforce tax claims should be sufficient to establish a presumption of insufficiency of assets and in such cases the Company Court should strike the company off the companies register upon application from the tax authority, without any further investigation. The idea was finally discarded for fear of fraud, since the powers of the tax authority are limited compared to those of the liquidator and do not permit a full assessment of the debtor's financial situation. In particular, the tax authority is not in a position to discover potentially avoidable transactions or investigate directors' past actions potentially amounting to wrongful trading.

Thus there will be a cohabitation of the floating lien and the floating charge in the new Hungarian Civil Code. For further details see N. Csizmazia, "Reform of the Hungarian Law of Security Rights in Movable Property" (2008) 1 Juridica International 181, 197.

[31] IA § 57(1).

[32] This is not a uniquely Hungarian situation. In the Netherlands, approximately 85 per cent of all liquidation proceedings are terminated for insufficiency of assets to cover the administrative expenses. Cf. R.J. Blom, Kernboekje faillissement, surseance en schuldsanering 2004/2005, Kluwer 2004, 151.

[33] IA § 63/B.

[34] These figures have been given by the Hungarian Association of Insolvency Practitioners (www.foe.hu).

[35] See e.g. Dutch Insolvency Act (Faillissementswet) Art. 16, Czech Insolvency Act (Act 182 of 30 March 2006) s. 144, Spanish Insolvency Act (Ley concursal) Art. 176.

Length of Liquidation Proceedings

Liquidation proceedings also tend to be extremely lengthy. A major problem in this respect is that the IA allows one year for the lodging of proofs of debt. More precisely, there are two deadlines for the submission of claims to the liquidator. Claims submitted after 40 days, but within one year from the public notice of the opening of the proceedings, are not extinguished, but merely postponed to claims submitted within 40 days. Only claims submitted later than one year from the opening of the proceedings are extinguished. Also tax authorities have one year for the control of the final tax declaration of the company in liquidation. As a result of these two factors, not even simplified liquidation proceedings where there is no reasonable prospect of any distribution to creditors can be concluded before the expiry of one year.

The excessive length of Hungarian liquidation proceedings has also led to Hungary's condemnation by the European Court of Human Rights for violation of Article 6 of the European Convention on Human Rights. In Bíró v. Hungary (2006)[36] and Hilti v. Hungary (2007)[37] the Court held that a liquidation still pending after 11 years (in Bíró v. Hungary) and 9 years (in Hilti v. Hungary) amounted to the violation of a creditor's right to a fair trial. However, the Court rejected the applicants' claims for substantial amounts in respect of pecuniary damage in both cases, and awarded them only €10,000 and €6,000 respectively, on an equitable basis, for non-pecuniary damages. These sums apparently do not motivate the Hungarian legislator to try to shorten the length of liquidation proceedings and avoid further condemnations by the ECHR.

Insufficient Creditor Control over the Liquidation Proceeding

A fundamental problem with the liquidation proceeding is that creditors are often not in a position to influence the course of events. First of all, creditors cannot nominate a liquidator or apply for the removal/replacement of the court-appointed liquidator. Second, in many cases the IA confers a right to control the actions of the liquidator on the creditors' committee, but the formation of a creditors' committee is not mandatory and in fact such a committee is rarely formed in the case of small and medium size companies. This results in the liquidator having much discretion e.g. in respect of the decision to run the debtor company as a going concern during the liquidation proceeding. According to the IA, the liquidator has to obtain the prior consent of the creditors' committee, if he intends to run the company as a going concern during the liquidation and the consent has to be renewed each year.

---

[36] Application No. 15652/04 (18/07/2006) (Second section).

[37] Application No. 25709/04 (09/10/2007) (Second section).

However, if there is no creditors' committee, the liquidator can take such a decision without any control, which often leads to the depletion of the assets.[38]

The remuneration scheme of liquidators (5 per cent of the proceeds arising from asset sales and the collection of outstanding receivables and an additional 2 per cent of sales revenues arising from operation as a going concern) also provides an incentive for the liquidators to operate the company as a going concern and delay the conclusion of proceedings even if it does not serve the best interests of pre-commencement creditors.[39]

Incentives for Owners and Directors to attempt to avoid Orderly Closure of Business Activities

In addition to the proceedings regulated in the IA, company law provides two alternative exit routes for companies:
* members' voluntary liquidation [*végelszámolási eljárás*]; and
* termination of a company with unknown registered office [*ismeretlen székhelyű cég megszüntetésére irányuló eljárás*].[40]

A members' voluntary liquidation is a proceeding available – in theory – only for solvent companies who intend to terminate their business and have enough assets to pay all their debts. However, these proceedings are often converted into insolvent liquidation with the companies' assets being dissipated. Therefore it is alleged that this proceeding is misused by insolvent companies to delay the opening of insolvency proceedings.[41] The main criticism against the rules of this procedure is that they confer weak control rights on creditors. Unlike liquidation, this proceeding is not conducted by a court-appointed insolvency professional. Instead, shareholders can appoint any person eligible for the office of director as a liquidator. Creditors are not entitled to nominate a liquidator. Nor is the company-appointed liquidator required to convene a meeting of creditors. Creditors are merely entitled to file a complaint with the Companies Court if they assert that the liquidator is in breach of his statutory duties. An other major cause for concern is that there is no statutory order of priority for the satisfaction of

---

[38] Other jurisdictions require authorisation either by the court or by the creditors' committee. Under French insolvency law le maintien de l'activité during liquidation is subject to court authorisation, given for a maximum of 3 (+3) months, but only if sale as a going concern is envisaged or if the continued trading is otherwise justified by public interest or by the creditors' interest. See Code de commerce, Art. L.641-10. According to the preliminary draft of the new Dutch Insolvency Act, the continuation of trading during liquidation is subject to the approval of the creditors' committee or that of the rechter-commissaris. See Voorontwerp-Insolventiewet, Art. 4.2.3a.

[39] For a detailed account of this phenomenon see J. Franks and Gy. Loranth, "A Study of Inefficient Going Concerns in Bankruptcy" (May 2005). CEPR Discussion Paper No. 5035. Available at SSRN: ssrn.com/abstract=774146 or www.jbs.cam.ac.uk/research/working_papers/2007/wp0703.pdf.

[40] Both are regulated in Act V of 2006 on Public Company Information, Company Registration and Members' Voluntary Liquidation.

[41] The credit rating company Coface Hungary has repeatedly stated in its periodical reports on Hungarian insolvency that this procedure is being misused by owners to transfer assets to new companies and defraud creditors. See e.g. www.fn.hu/vallalkozas/20070712/novekvo_korbetartozasok_vegelszamolasok_mogott/.

debts in a members' voluntary liquidation (on the assumption that the company is able to satisfy all its debts).

The proceeding known as "termination of a company with unknown registered office" raises even more concerns. If a company can no longer be found at its registered office, or the company's directors cannot be located or their address is deemed unknown (i.e. the director resides abroad and has no registered agent for the service of documents in Hungary), a notice is published in the Companies Gazette addressed to the company's members requesting them to restore lawful operations within 60 days. Simultaneously, a direct notice is given to members with more than 50 per cent of votes similarly requesting them to restore lawful operations. If the lawful operation is not restored, the Companies Court makes an order for the termination of the company. A search is performed by the Companies Court (in the public registers and via public notice in the Companies Gazette) to find out if there are any assets available for distribution among the creditors. If no assets are discovered, the company is struck off the register without formal liquidation.

According to the Companies Act, a person who acted as a director of a company in the year prior to the company's being struck off the register (in the above proceeding) is disqualified from holding the office of a company director for 2 years,[42] but this is again a provision existing only in the statute book, as no register of such directors is kept. There are similarly ineffective provisions on the unlimited liability of controlling shareholders of companies struck off the register (in the above proceeding) for the unpaid debts of the company.[43] The creditor invoking these provisions is required to prove that the company's unpaid debts were in excess of 50 per cent of the company's capital and reserves. However, the creditor is unlikely to be able to prove this, as there are usually no accounts filed by these "disappeared" directors and as a result it is impossible to find out the proportion of the total unpaid debt to the capital and reserves.

On the other hand, the establishment of new companies has recently become considerably cheaper and quicker. From 1 July 2008, electronic registration takes place within 1 hour in the simplified registration procedure (i.e. when template articles of association are used). Even if the registration takes place on the basis of paper documents, it does not take more than 15 days. The registration fees have also been significantly reduced: the fee is HUF 15,000 (≈ € 50) in the simplified electronic registration procedure irrespective of the legal form of the company. Minimum capital requirements have also been lowered: from 1 September 2007, a GmbH-style limited liability company can be established with HUF 500,000 (≈ € 1,725), a private company limited by shares with HUF 5 million (≈ € 17,240).

---

[42] Act IV of 2006 on Companies § 23(3).

[43] Act V of 2006 on Public Company Information, Company Registration and Members' Voluntary Liquidation § 93 and IA § 63/A.

The availability of alternative exit routes less controlled by the court and creditors, the lack of efficient rules on the accountability to creditors and finally the ease of setting up a new company all provide incentives for directors and shareholders to try to avoid the orderly closure of business activities by way of liquidation proceedings.

Lack of an Adequate Institutional Framework for the Regulation, Licensing and Oversight of the Insolvency Profession

The register of insolvency professionals ("IPs") is kept by the Ministry of Finance.[44] The Ministry decides when to issue calls for new applications, but no such call has been issued since 1997. This does not cause problems for two reasons. First, only firms [45] can be licensed as IPs, the individuals employed by IP firms do not have to be authorised.[46] Second, IP firms (or shares in IP firms) can be sold together with the licences issued by the Ministry of Finance, the licences being regarded as transferable patrimonial rights. Therefore a change in the ownership of an IP firm does not entail a need for new registration. This raises some concerns, as the reassessment of compliance with the statutory requirements is thereby avoided.

Currently, the individuals acting on behalf of IP firms have to be either lawyers admitted to the bar, economists or auditors registered with the Hungarian Chamber of Auditors, but there is no statutory requirement to attend a specialized training course or to pass an examination set by a professional body. From 2010, this will change: an additional requirement of a specialized postgraduate diploma will apply.

However, there is no monitoring of compliance with qualification requirements. There is no government agency comparable to the Insolvency Service (England & Wales), the Accountant in Bankruptcy (Scotland) or the Conseil national des administrateurs judiciaires et des mandataires judiciaires (France). Nor are IP firms required by law to be members of a professional body, though in practice IP firms are usually members of the Association of Insolvency Practitioners (FOE).[47]

---

[44] Government Decree No. 114/2006 (V. 12.) on the Register of Liquidators.

[45] The firm has to be either a limited liability company (akin to the German GmbH) or a private company limited by shares.

[46] To get a licence, IP firms must employ (or have a contract with) at least 2 lawyers, 2 economists and 2 auditors. The firm designated by the court as liquidator appoints one of these individuals to act on its behalf.

[47] See www.foe.hu.

Insolvency Law Teaching and Scholarship in Hungary

The reform of insolvency law is not an easy task in any jurisdiction. However, in Hungary, the situation is worsened by a lack of academic interest in this field.

First of all, the subject has a rather low standing in the curriculum of most law faculties. A look at the websites of Hungarian law faculties shows the following picture for 2008-2009: In the undergraduate programme [48] of the probably most prestigious Hungarian law faculty (ELTE, Budapest) insolvency law is only offered as an optional course of the Department of Economics, although it is also part of a "lightweight" obligatory course on Non-Contentious Civil Procedure. The other two "older" law faculties (Pécs, Szeged) also teach insolvency law only as part of the course on Non-Contentious Civil Procedure. The situation is not significantly better at most of the "younger" law faculties founded (or re-founded) after 1989. The University of Győr offers only an optional course on "Insolvency Law in Practice". The University of Debrecen offers an obligatory course on Commercial Law, but insolvency law is not among the topics dealt with. Commercial Law is an obligatory course at the Law Faculty of the Pázmány Catholic University of Budapest, but insolvency law is the subject of only one lecture. The undergraduate curriculum of the Law Faculty of the University of Miskolc is the exception: it includes not only an obligatory course in Commercial Law with three lectures on Corporate Insolvency Law, but also an optional course (running through two semesters) on Corporate Insolvency Law.[49] In addition to the undergraduate programmes, three faculties (Budapest, Pécs, Miskolc) offer part-time postgraduate courses leading to diplomas in commercial law, these courses including some lectures on insolvency law.

It seems safe to conclude that Hungarian law faculties, with the exception of Miskolc, assign only a marginal role to insolvency law. This is possibly the heritage of the Socialist period when insolvency was treated as a non-existent phenomenon, the insolvency legislation was repealed and insolvency law was not on the legal curriculum at all. The relegation of insolvency law to the law of civil procedure (at the three older faculties of ELTE Budapest, Pécs and Szeged) may have something to do with the German-Austrian view of insolvency law as part of the Law of Civil Procedure (Zivilverfahrensrecht). The decision of many younger law faculties to separate the teaching of civil law and commercial law (despite the non-existence of a separate commercial code) may have had some

---

[48] The undergraduate programme of law faculties is designed for 5 years (10 semesters). Examinations are taken at the end of each semester. In addition, a supervised thesis of approximately 30.000 words has to be submitted and four final examinations (Civil Law, Criminal Law, Constitutional & Administrative Law, Philosophy of Law) have to be passed.

[49] The pre-eminence of the Law Faculty of Miskolc in teaching and research in the field of insolvency law is also confirmed by the fact that only two papers on insolvency law have been awarded a prize in the bi-annual nationwide competition (OTDK) of Hungarian law students between 2001 and 2007 and both have been written under the supervision of a professor of the Law Faculty of Miskolc. See www.otdt.hu.

beneficial impact on the ranking of insolvency law in the curriculum, although this is only clear in one law faculty.

The academic literature on insolvency law [50] is also scarce. The books published after 1989 on insolvency law are commentaries of the existing legislation and case law, but provide no insight into the policy issues and do not aim at building a theoretical framework for the study of insolvency law. Only one of these books [51] contains some comparative observations and only one of them takes a critical stance to the current legislation. [52] Unfortunately, none of them is comparable to the standard pre-WWII Hungarian textbook on insolvency law, [53] which comprised two volumes: one on "formal insolvency law" (i.e. the procedural aspects of insolvency law) and another on "material insolvency law" (i.e. the commercial law side of insolvency law), was rich in historic and comparative details and presented the subject as a coherent whole, with an emphasis on the underlying principles. Monographic works on specific issues of insolvency law have not been published since 1989.

Articles on insolvency law rarely appear in legal journals. [54] The legal journal *Gazdaság és jog* [Economy and Law], where articles on insolvency law are most likely to be published, contained only 26 articles on insolvency law in the period between 1989 and 2008. The most widely read *Magyar jog* [Hungarian Law] contained only 19 articles during the same period (3 being translations of articles published by foreign authors in foreign journals). The total number of articles published on insolvency law in Hungarian legal journals between 1989 and 2008 is between 70 and 80, [55] but many of these merely describe the successive amendments of the Insolvency Act and do not aim to contribute to the discussion of a particular topic.

---

[50] Leaving aside the out-of-date commentaries, four books should be mentioned: A. Csőke et al., A csődtörvény magyarázata [The Commentary of the Insolvency Act], Budapest 2003, L. Juhász, Csődjog - A magyar csődjog kézikönyve [Insolvency Law – A Handbook of Hungarian Insolvency Law], Pécs 2003, A. Boóc, I. Sándor, M. Tóth et al., Csődjog [Insolvency Law], 2nd edn, Budapest 2007, L. Juhász, A magyar fizetésképtelenségi jog kézikönyve [The Handbook of Hungarian Insolvency Law] Miskolc 2008.

[51] A. Boóc, I. Sándor, M. Tóth et al., Csődjog [Insolvency Law], 2nd edn, Budapest 2007.

[52] A. Csőke et al., A csődtörvény magyarázata [The Commentary of the Insolvency Act], Budapest 2003.

[53] I. Apáthy, A magyar csődjog rendszere [The System of Hungarian Insolvency Law] Vols. 1-2. Budapest 1887–1888. Apáthy was not only the author of a textbook on insolvency law, but also the principal draftsman of the 1881 Insolvency Act.

[54] The following figures are based on a search in the on-line database MATARKA (www.matarka.hu). I searched for articles in legal journals that contain in their title or among the keywords describing the subject-matter of the article the Hungarian equivalents of the words "insolvency" [fizetésképtelenség], "bankruptcy" [csőd] or "liquidation" [felszámolás], or variations of these words. I also checked each result of the search since the Hungarian word for bankruptcy [csőd] may simply mean "failure", while the Hungarian word for liquidation [felszámolás] may simply mean "abolition".

[55] Depending on whether only Hungarian contributions or also Hungarian translations of articles published in foreign journals are taken into account.

Empirical research is almost completely missing, [56] hard data on the number, the length and the costs of proceedings or the returns to creditors are not readily available. [57] The Hungarian government does not seem to feel the need to collect and analyse statistical data when preparing new legislation or evaluating the impact of previous reforms.

The lack of significant academic interest and research may not have been the main factor, but has definitely contributed to the low quality of Hungarian legislation in the field of insolvency law.

[56] I have found only two empirical studies on Hungarian insolvency law. One was published in 1996 and analysed the application of the IA in the early post-transition period: Ch.W. Gray, S. Schlorke and M. Szanyi, "A csődtörvény tapasztalatai Magyarországon 1992-1993", 1996 (XLIII) Közgazdasági Szemle, 403-419. The other was done by researchers of English universities more recently: J. Franks and Gy. Loranth, "A Study of Inefficient Going Concerns in Bankruptcy" (n 39). In addition A. Csőke, "Gondolatok az új fizetésképtelenségi törvény szükségességéről a Csődtörvény statisztikája tükrében" 2002 (49) Magyar jog 2, 86-95 analyses statistical data in coming to her suggestions regarding a new insolvency act.

[57] Private companies (e.g. Coface Hungary) and the Association of Insolvency Practitioners collect and publish data on the number of insolvency proceedings.

Chapter 3

A Dual Law for Companies in Financial Distress

Karin Luttikhuis

Introduction

In Europe, as well as in the Netherlands, little empirical research exists into the efficiency of the Bankruptcy Act (*Faillissementswet*). The Dutch legislature has now been working for dozens of years on revising insolvency legislation to ensure that non-viable businesses liquidate effectively and efficiently and viable businesses restructure effectively and efficiently. The legislature and Supreme Court (Hoge Raad) translate this into three goals: maximisation of the proceeds for the joint creditors and preservation of business and employment.[1] But in the Netherlands, it is not known whether insolvency law is effective and efficient, nor how we can achieve this. In this paper, I give an account of the research into the problem that it is unknown in the Netherlands whether the insolvency procedure and/or informal restructuring achieve these goals (efficiently) and what policy or rules the legislature needs to formulate to allow these procedures to better achieve these goals. This problem is studied by using file research and research of literature and case law. The file research consists of a study of court files of all 4,167 company insolvencies terminated in 2004.[2] The scope of the research and this paper compel me to limit myself to a description of the main conclusions and recommendations of this study.[3]

---

[1] See e.g. the legal history: G.W. Van der Feltz, Geschiedenis van de Wet op het faillissement en de surseance van betaling, 1896, p. 27, 339, 371 ff. and 428; and also the judgments of the Supreme Court of 24 February 1995 (Sigmacon II)(NJ/Dutch case law) 1996, 472) and of 19 April 1996 (Maclou/Curatoren Van Schuppen)(NJ/Dutch case law) 1996, 727). I refer to A.P.K. Luttikhuis, Corporate recovery, de weg naar effectief insolventierecht, 2007, p. 26 ff., for more information about these goals and the discussion in the doctrine.

[2] Because of the limited scope of this paper, for a Dutch description of the methodology used, please refer to A.P.K. Luttikhuis, Corporate recovery, de weg naar effectief insolventierecht, 2007, Chapter 1 (Dutch) and for an English description of the methodology, to A.P.K. Luttikhuis, "Is Corporate Insolvency Law Effective and Efficient?", International Insolvency Review, Volume 17, 2008, issue 3, section two.

[3] The study is published in the Netherlands in various books and papers. From 2003, I have conducted large-scale research in collaboration with Statistics Netherlands into the problem that it is unknown whether the insolvency procedure and/or informal restructuring achieve these goals (efficiently), and what policy the legislature should formulate to enable these procedures to achieve these goals better and more efficiently. The research on the relatively minor importance of the insolvency procedure and the great importance of informal restructuring was first published in Insolventierecht in cijfers en modellen: werkgelegenheid en toezicht, (Insolvency law in figures and models: employment and supervision), The Hague: Boom Juridische Uitgevers (legal publishers), 2006. This book was published in digital form for the first time on 15 March 2006 on the website of Statistics Netherlands (CBS); A.P.K.

Insolvency Procedure is of less Social Importance than expected; Goals barely achieved

We see that in revising insolvency legislation, the Dutch legislature and doctrine focus mainly on the formal procedures, especially the insolvency procedure. High requirements are set on it and the expectations of it are high. In the course of the years, in addition to its original function, maximisation of the proceeds for the joint creditors, the insolvency procedure has been given several social functions, such as preservation of business and employment, combating the abuse of insolvency law and perhaps in the future also combating insolvency fraud. The question whether the insolvency procedure can fulfil those major functions is not answered: Is the insolvency procedure indeed socially relevant? Nor has the question been answered of who should finance the costs of achieving those social goals. Insolvency in itself is, after all, a private matter of a debtor and various creditors and it is not automatically a fact that this has to be pursued at the expense of individuals.

The study of insolvencies that ended in 2004 shows that the insolvency procedure does not succeed in achieving its original goal: maximisation of the proceeds for the joint creditors. Various types of creditors received a payment in only a small percentage of the insolvencies. For instance, in the years 1996 to 2004, the unsecured and other preferential creditors received a (partial) payment in respectively 8% and 10% on average of the terminated corporate insolvencies. In those years, the Tax and Customs Administration and the Employee Insurance Agency received a (partial) payment in 30% on average of the corporate insolvencies. It is also evident that the recovery rate of the unsecured and other preferential creditors was low: over the years 1996 to 2004, this rate was respectively 3.2% and 6.3% on average. The recovery rate of the Tax and Customs Administration over those years was 9.6% on average and that of the Employee Insurance Agency 11.5% (both relate only to their preferential claims).

Before making a statement on the extent to which the insolvency procedure achieves its social goals, I examined whether the insolvency procedure is socially relevant.[4] I had to limit this broad term in this study, in which I use the following indicators: the number of companies that used the insolvency procedure, the size of the insolvent companies, the number of employees in service at the time of the insolvency order, the number of businesses that were (partially) preserved and the presence or not of a negative corporate estate. The study shows that the insolvency procedure is not as socially relevant as we presume. The companies that become insolvent are relatively small and had relatively few employees in service at the

Luttikhuis, Corporate recovery, de weg naar effectief insolventierecht (Corporate recovery, the way towards effective insolvency law), Amsterdam: <corporate-recovery.org> 2007. The latter book contains the entire study; an English translation will be published shortly.

[4] See A.P.K. Luttikhuis, op. cit. 2007, chapter two.

The Intersection of Insolvency and Company Laws

time of the insolvency order. There were negative corporate estates in 75% of the insolvencies and businesses were saved in only 6.3% by way of a restart. These figures from the total study deviate sharply from the earlier sub-studies by the Hugo Sinzheimer Institute from 2005 (HSI)[5] and by the Business & Law Research Centre (OO&R) from 2001.[6] On the basis of those sub-studies, they arrived at a percentage of 63-66%. These studies do not represent the whole of insolvencies. Furthermore, the businesses were preserved in only 0.55% of the insolvencies by way of an arrangement. This is in contrast to the earlier study by the Business and Law Research Centre from 2001, which arrived at 8%. The number of insolvencies (4,167) is substantially smaller than the number of companies that try to remedy their financial problems by informal restructuring, which numbered 24,500 in 2002-2003. Further research will have to provide more certainty regarding these numbers.

As it is evident from the foregoing that the social importance of the insolvency procedure is less than was presumed, it is not surprising that the insolvency procedure achieves its social goals to only a limited extent. I stated above that in the insolvency procedure, only a small percentage of the insolvent companies preserved their business. Before I can make a statement as to whether the social interest of "preservation of *business in general*" is achieved, I need to relate the research results to the total number of companies in the Netherlands. The 285 companies that were preserved during insolvency constitute only 0.41 per thousand of the average number of companies in the Netherlands from 1996 to 2004. The number of companies that preserved their business in insolvency also remains negligibly small if one relates this number to the aforementioned 24,000 informal corporate restructurings. The study by Van Amsterdam from 2004 shows that 48-61% of these were successful.[7] If one starts from a conservative estimate, the number of successful informal restructurings comes to about half of 24,500, which is 12,250. This means that the 285 businesses that remained preserved (in part) are still only 2.3% of the number of successful restructurings. The insolvency procedure therefore hardly achieves the social goal of preservation of *business in general.*

Closely connected with the goal of preservation of business is the goal of preservation of employment. In the insolvency procedure, in principle, employment can only be preserved if business is preserved. Before this study was conducted, it was not known how many employees and therefore how much employment was involved in an insolvency procedure. It is evident from the research results that in the insolvencies, a total of 19,253 employees were in service at the time of the insolvency order. Of these employees, 15.4% (2,971)

---

[5] R. Knegt, R.J. Popma and I. Zaal, Fraude en misbruik bij faillissement, Amsterdam Hugo Sinzheimer Instituut (HSI), 2005, p. 75 ff.

[6] O. Couwenberg, S.C.J.J. Kortmann and N.E.D. Faber, De efficiëntie van de Faillissementstwet, Onderzoekscentrum Onderneming & Recht (Business & Law Research Centre)(OO&R) 2001, p. 51.

[7] A.M. van Amsterdam, Insolventie in economisch perspectief, Den Haag 2004, p. 229 ff. He uses the definition "success for society", by which he means that the business, whether or not after restructuring (including sale or divestment of divisions) continues to exist and makes a meaningful contribution to commerce (p. 230).

employees kept their jobs. This means that at most 16,282 employees lost their jobs as a result of an insolvency. To what extent are these numbers on the basis of which it must be established that the existing employment in the Netherlands is seriously threatened by insolvencies, and therefore a receiver should include the social interest of *employment in general* in his considerations? To be able to answer this, I relate the number of employees who lost their jobs to employment in the Netherlands. This number constitutes 2.2 per thousand and is therefore a very small part of existing "employment" in general. I note in this regard that it is unknown whether the employees who lost their jobs in the insolvencies were employed fulltime or for a few hours at the time of the insolvency order.

If one considers only the employees who lost their jobs in insolvencies in which the business was transferred during the insolvency, the insolvency procedure is even less important for the preservation of employment in general. The research results show that although there was only a small percentage of restarts (in 6.3% of the insolvencies, in this limited number of cases, more than half of the employees kept their jobs (55.4%). A restart was made in only 241 insolvencies of companies that had employees in service. Together, they had 5,363 employees in service. This is 0.728 per thousand of the total employment in the Netherlands. In reality, this number is probably even lower, because of those 5,363 employees, 2,971 were transferred along with the business. Consequently, the number of workers who were not transferred is still only 2,393, which comes down to only 0.324 per thousand of the total employment, whereby it should be noted that it is unknown whether these employment contracts were for a fixed term or indefinite time. Apart from the far-reaching consequences of the insolvency for the individual employees who lose their jobs because of it, this percentage seems too low to maintain the position that in insolvencies, the acts of the receiver or delegated judge can contribute substantially to the social interest of "employment" in general. Based on this, I conclude that the insolvency procedure does not achieve its goal of preserving *employment in general*, or achieves it only to a very limited extent.

The Efficiency of Social Goals is Unknown

Apart from the question whether the insolvency procedure achieves its goals of preservation of business and employment, it is not clear whether this is done efficiently. The costs of achieving these goals are unknown. The goals of maximisation of the proceeds for the joint creditors is a net goal, in the sense that the costs of achieving this goal are already taken into account in the final payments to the creditors. Preservation of business and employment are gross goals. In this study, I have examined the extent to which they are achieved, but the costs of achieving these social goals are unknown. For instance, it is not clear whether the costs of keeping a job are, so to speak, one million or nil Euros. It is known, however, that these costs are in principle borne by the creditors, while they do not necessarily receive the benefits.

Little Abuse of Insolvency Law

The study[8] shows that companies do not use the insolvency procedure on a large scale to avoid protecting their employees. Of the two instruments in the insolvency procedure that pertain to combating the abuse of insolvency law for the purpose of protecting employees, Article 67 (2) of the Bankruptcy Act does not operate effectively. The operation of the other instrument, Article 13a of the Bankruptcy Act is beyond the scope of this study.

A possibility to combat abuse of insolvency law further is to amend the employment law relating to the termination of employment contracts. Prevailing employment law does not take account of the fact that interests have to be weighed differently in companies in financial difficulties from those in healthy companies. If a company is in financial difficulties, the employees' interests have to be represented in a different way from those of a healthy company. In that situation, not only the changed interests of the employees and the interests of the debtors should be included in the weighing of interests, but also the interests of the creditors. Employment law that takes account of the different weighing of interests in companies in financial difficulties could see to it that companies are better able to restructure and do not have to use the insolvency procedure in order to restructure. This would increase the chances of employees of companies in financial difficulties of keeping their jobs.

Barely achieving Goals is not due to Instruments that prevent the Consequences of Creditor Prejudice or pertain to Supervision

As the insolvency procedure achieves its goals only to a limited extent, I examined whether this is due to the operation of several instruments of the insolvency procedure which are currently the centre of attention: the instruments by which receivers can take action against prejudicing of creditors and the instruments for the purpose of supervising the procedure. Prior to the study, it was not known whether these instruments had an effect on achievement of the goals of the insolvency procedure.

It can be concluded from the study of the instruments by which receivers can take action against prejudicing of creditors[9] that the question of how these instruments work is limited to 10% of the insolvencies of natural persons and 19% of the insolvencies of legal persons in which creditors were prejudiced. In addition, the operation of these instruments is further limited to somewhat more than half of those insolvencies. In almost half of the cases, there were insufficient possibilities for recovery or funds in the corporate estate to finance an action by the receiver. It is important as well that, in principle, these instruments can only have an effect on the maximisation of the proceeds of the joint creditors.

[8] See A.P.K. Luttikhuis, op. cit. 2007, chapter three.

[9] The study is published in the Netherlands in various books and papers, among others in A.P.K. Luttikhuis and R.E. Timmermans, "Effecten van schuldeisersbenadeling onder de huidige Faillissementswet", and A.P.K. Luttikhuis, "Conclusies en aanbevelingen", in: A.P.K. Luttikhuis and R.E. Timmermans (eds), Insolventierecht in cijfers en modellen, schuldeisersbenadeling en conclusies, Den Haag: Boom Juridische Uitgevers 2007 and A.P.K. Luttikhuis, op. cit. 2007, chapter four.

The receiver used one of the aforementioned instruments in approximately one fourth of the insolvencies of natural persons in which creditors were prejudiced (27%). The receiver took action in approximately a third of the insolvencies of legal persons in which creditors were prejudiced (39%). In cases where receivers ultimately did use such an instrument, this was ineffective in the lion's share of the insolvencies, as the use of one of these instruments by the receiver did not result in payment of the creditors. For instance, an action by a receiver in 82 per cent (natural persons) and 88 per cent (legal persons) of the corporate insolvencies in which the receiver had used an instrument did not result in payment of the unsecured creditors. The reason for this was that in that percentage of insolvencies, the unsecured creditors as a whole did not receive any payment. It is not known whether this was due to the costs of using the instrument, which are fully payable by the creditors, or to a lack of assets.

Informal Restructuring

Furthermore, it is evident[10] that the legislature has concentrated too much on the insolvency procedure instead of informal restructuring. Although informal restructuring is largely an unexplored territory, it is evident from this study and the current state of knowledge that there is more room in it for achieving the aforementioned goals and that the social interest of this procedure is considerably greater. The estimated number of companies involved in informal restructuring is much larger than the number of companies involved annually in an insolvency procedure. The percentage of successful restructurings compared to the percentage of successful restarts in insolvency is much higher than believed until recently. Furthermore, relatively more employment is preserved in informal restructurings than in insolvency procedures. In addition, in informal restructurings, the creditors (who must all agree to the settlement) receive payment more often. The importance of informal restructuring is expected to continue increasing in the future, as the Insolvency Law Committee intends to limit the influence of the separatists in the new insolvency legislation. The bank-dominated system in the Netherlands, with a relative concentration of loan capital, was already a fertile environment for informal restructuring, as the providers of loan capital de facto dominated the process instead of a receiver or administrator. Because of the weaker position of separatists in the formal procedures, the banks are expected to assert their influence more often in the preliminary process so that companies will decide on informal restructuring.

On the basis of literature and theoretical research, I come to the conclusion that prevailing employment law relating to the termination of employment contracts impedes informal restructuring. At present, there is only one type of employment law which is applicable to healthy companies and companies in financial difficulties.

---

[10] See A.P.K. Luttikhuis, Insolventierecht in cijfers en modellen: werkgelegenheid en toezicht, (Insolvency law in figures and models: employment and supervision), The Hague: Boom Juridische Uitgevers (legal publishers), 2006 and A.P.K. Luttikhuis, op. cit. 2007, chapter 7.

The Intersection of Insolvency and Company Laws

It is important to make a distinction regarding the termination of employment contract between companies that are and are not in financial difficulties, whether or not a formal insolvency procedure is followed. In the employment law applicable to a company in financial difficulties, account could then be taken of the changed interests of the employees as a result of the insolvency of the company where they work and of the interests of the creditors. In the employment law applicable to a healthy company, the present weighing of interests between employees and employer could continue to take a central place. In short, "dual employment law" should be enacted in relation to the termination of employment contracts. This could improve informal restructuring.

Another important conclusion is that no form of supervision exists now of the players in informal restructuring, while it deals with relatively major interests and, as said, with a situation in which the interests of the principal players do not always coincide with the collective interest. There is a big difference between the success ratios of the company bank and the company. In certain situations, the individual interests of the company bank and/or the Tax and Customs Administration do not run parallel to the collective interest. I recommend some form of supervision.

Recommendations

Based on the research, I make a number of recommendations presented below.

Informal Restructuring is very Important

The legislature wants to see to it that non-viable companies in financial difficulties liquidate effectively and efficiently and the viable companies effectively and efficiently restructure. To achieve this, it should not focus its attention only on formal insolvency procedures, but especially on informal restructuring.

Little research has been done on informal reorganisation. Further research is necessary into the extent, description and analysis of informal restructuring and the problems occurring during it. Attention needs to be paid to employment law and some form of supervision of the principal players in this procedure: the bank and the Tax and Customs Administration. In an impetus for a debate over supervision, I proposed appointing an undisclosed delegated judge. It should also be considered whether effective insolvency law requires a distinction between insolvency law according to the size of companies and the level of assets present and whether insolvency law should be included in a separate act or in the existing legislation relating to employment law, tax law etc. I propose using the term "corporate recovery" for the solving of financial difficulties in informal restructuring. This is positive, forward looking and makes insolvency discussible.

Dual Employment Law

The European legislature has required the Dutch legislature to take measures to prevent the abuse of insolvency law with a view to the position of employees. It is evident from the research that companies do not use insolvency law on a large scale to rid themselves of employees. It appears that employment law, as it applies outside the insolvency procedure, may actually be partly responsible for companies becoming insolvent. Prevailing employment law can impede informal restructuring because it does not take account of the changed interests of the employees of a company in financial difficulties, nor of the interests of the creditors.

I recommend enacting dual employment law in relation to the termination of employment contracts. Employment law relating to healthy companies and employment law pertaining to companies in financial difficulties. In the employment law pertaining to healthy companies, the current weighing of interests between the less powerful employees and the employer can continue to take a central place. The employment law pertaining to companies in financial difficulties should focus on the changed weighing of interests. Employment law that takes account of the changed interests of employees of companies in financial difficulties could see to it that companies can restructure better and do not have to use the insolvency procedure in order to do so. This increases the chances of employees of companies in financial difficulties to keep their jobs.

Dual Supervision

The doctrine and the legislature focus on supervision in the insolvency procedure, as is evident from the debates over the quality of the delegated judge, the latter's actual supervision and the receiver's fee. The preliminary conclusion can be drawn on the basis of the research that there is no question of failing supervision in the insolvency procedure. Creditors, for instance, appear to make little use of the means at their disposal to supervise the insolvency procedure. The preliminary conclusion can be drawn from this that there is no question of failing supervision or that receivers properly administer corporate estates and therefore amendments to the instruments pertaining to supervision in the insolvency procedure will not enable the insolvency procedure to (better) achieve its goals. Further research should nevertheless be conducted into supervision by the delegated judge and creditors in the insolvency procedure to rule out that the reasons why creditors do not make much use of the existing instruments at their disposal are: lack of familiarity with these instruments or inaction in an insolvency procedure because the costs exceed the benefits for the creditors.

The research has shown that the lack of supervision of the assets falling outside the insolvency procedure is more important than the debate over supervision in the insolvency procedure. Based on the current state of research, informal restructuring is more important than the insolvency procedure and enables the three goals to be achieved to a greater extent than in the insolvency procedure. But this is not supervised at all. In informal restructuring, the bank and the Tax and Customs Administration are the principal players. In that procedure, they can in principle pursue their individual interests, whether or not in conflict with the collective interests. Prior and subsequent supervision can be chosen.

In informal restructuring, the usual supervision and control systems do not have an effect on the company management because the company bank actually takes over the management. It is therefore important to create an adequate supervision regime.[11] The corporate governance system of a company in financial difficulties differs from that of a healthy company. In healthy companies, the shareholders are first and foremost and supervision relates to the management. In companies in financial difficulties, the creditors' interests are in the foreground and supervision of the company bank is also important. "Dual law" is involved here as well. Some form of supervision is expected to increase the effectiveness of this procedure. Further research into this is necessary.

As an impetus for a further debate over forms of supervision in informal restructuring, I describe below the undisclosed delegated judge as supervisor. In choosing a form of supervision, one should first choose between prior supervision and subsequent supervision by way of liability standards. A disadvantage of the latter form of supervision is that liability standards entail much uncertainty for the players involved and have a stigmatising effect.[12] A form of prior supervision is opting for an undisclosed delegated judge. In the event of insolvency, the debtor could opt for an undisclosed delegated judge who supervises informal restructuring for the benefit of the joint creditors. Opting for an undisclosed delegated judge could be made mandatory if a company has to report its inability to pay to the Tax and Customs Administration[13] and if the company bank places the company with its special administration department. This is the time that a breach of the equality of creditors is prevented in favour of the principal players. It also enables the information advantage of the principal players to be shared for the benefit of the collective. This makes room to strive for social interests. Insolvency law is precisely intended to guarantee the equality of creditors. It also ensures the requisite timeliness. In other cases, the undisclosed delegated judge is voluntary. A choice can also be made to have an accountant expert apply for the undisclosed delegated judge. The accountant of a company in financial difficulties often finds himself in a field of conflicting interests.[14] If, for example, he includes a discontinuity section in the audit report, the company will soon be liquidated. If he does not do so, he could be held liable. If the accountant of a company in financial difficulties is able to request an undisclosed delegated judge for that company, this could break through the impasse. An undisclosed delegated judge would enable informal restructuring to take place in the requisite privacy.[15] It is important for a delegated judge to have commercial as well as legal insight. He

---

[11] Cf. e.g. J.W. Winter, "Doorstart, waarheen?" TVVS 1997, p. 207.

[12] Cf. e.g. J.W. Winter, op. cit. 2007, p. 208-214.

[13] Cf. MDW-Eindrapport 2001 p. 8. There is a need for an early warning system.

[14] Cf. A.M. van Amsterdam, op. cit. 2004, p. 141 ff.

[15] Cf. e.g. H.P.J. Ophof, "Faillissement, surseance van betaling en continuïteit van de onderneming", in: D.H. Beukenhorst et al. (ed.), Het faillissement in de tijd van Molengraaff en nu, Preliminary advice of the Commercial Law Association ("Vereeniging Handelsrecht"), Zwolle 1993

or she could be a lawyer with commercial knowledge or an accountant or another professional with commercial as well as legal knowledge. The latter could act as a deputy judge. The undisclosed delegated judge is a supervisor of the collective process of informal restructuring. Depending on how this is worked out, the appointment of an undisclosed judge could be an efficient and effective form of dispute resolution for the stakeholders. One possibility is to have the debtor pay a registry fee, the amount of which would depend on the size of the corporate estate, in order to finance reliance on the delegated judge. Finances permitting, the undisclosed delegated judge could also be assisted by an expert.

Reconsideration of Social Interests

In the insolvency procedure, different social interests have to be pursued. Not just the preservation of business and employment, but also combating the abuse of law, and in the future perhaps insolvency fraud as well. These substantial social interests are totally unrelated to the actual interest of the insolvency procedure, whereby "business" and therefore "employment" is preserved in only a very limited number of cases.

The research has shed a different light on the social importance of the insolvency procedure. It shows that social goals are brought up for discussion in few insolvencies, let alone achieved. If the legislature nevertheless wants to strive for social goals in an insolvency procedure and these interests conflict with the interests of the joint creditors, it is first of all important for the legislature to conduct further research into the costs of striving for these interests. This could make not only the benefits of the goals, but also their costs clear. Insight into this is lacking at present.

The cost-benefit side is already clear in the goal of striving for maximisation of the joint proceeds. The payments the creditors ultimately receive are, after all, a result of the costs and benefits of achieving this goal. This is not the case in the preservation of employment and business or the condition of combating the abuse of insolvency law. These are often wrongly equated with only the number of jobs and businesses that are preserved and the number of times abuse is combated. The costs of this are not known. It is known, however that, in principle, the creditors are the ones who bear these costs. If further research is conducted into this, and it shows that the costs are relatively high, the legislature should answer the question of who should bear these costs. The costs of striving for social goals should in principle be payable by the those who benefit from them. This is usually society. Based on this idea, it is also possible to charge these costs to a group of creditors who benefit from the pursuit of those social interests. These are usually the Tax and Customs Administration and the Employee Insurance Agency. This would prevent the costs of the social interests from being charged to a random group of creditors. At present, the costs of the social interests may usually be charged to the weakest group of creditors: the unsecured and preferential (commercial) creditors.[16]

An example of possible future legislation in which a new social interest is added to the insolvency procedure at the expense of the creditors is insolvency fraud. In for example the Draft Insolvency Bill,[17] it is provided that the receiver is obliged to inform the delegated judge when there is a reasonable suspicion that someone has committed an offence. [18]According to the Draft Insolvency Bill, the delegated judge is able to instruct the receiver to report the offence (Article 4.3.4.2 of the Draft Insolvency Bill). In Article 6.1.2 of the Draft Insolvency Bill, it is stated that the costs of the receiver are payable by the State when the estate does not have sufficient financial resources, but the Draft Insolvency Bill does not mention that if the estate has sufficient financial resources, it is up to the creditors to finance this public interest.

The comments above on the social goals in the insolvency procedure would also apply if the legislature were to focus on informal restructuring and wished to strive for social interests in doing so.

Instruments to combat Creditor Prejudice

The research shows that the insolvency procedure achieves its goals only to a limited extent. I then examined whether the insolvency procedure could better achieve its goals if the instruments intended to prevent the consequences of prejudicing of creditors were amended. The research results show that the presence of prejudicing of creditors has a (minor) adverse effect on the goal of maximisation of the proceeds and hardly any effect on the other two goals. It is also evident that if the receiver takes actions, this may not be financially favourable for the various types of creditors in the lion's share of insolvencies because they do not receive any payment in that case. If the legislature wants to improve the instruments, I recommend that further research be conducted first into the causes of the failure of the current instruments to function. Further research will have to show whether or not the effectiveness of the instruments to combat prejudicing of creditors can be improved. This research could, in principle, be limited to the corporate insolvencies in which prejudicing of creditors occurred (10-19% (natural persons and legal persons)), except for almost half of those insolvencies in which the receiver did not take action owing to lack of funds and/or recovery possibilities (45-48% (natural persons and legal persons)). It is important for the legislature to recognise that here, too, the creditor are the ones who bear the costs of the receiver's use of the instruments.

---

[16] I explained this in A.P.K. Luttikhuis, loc cit 2004, p. 74-83.

[17] The Draft Insolvency Bill was presented by the current Insolvency Law Committee to the Minister of Justice in November 2007.

[18] Art. 4.2.14 Draft Insolvency Bill, see www.justitie.nl.

We have seen that the insolvency procedure hardly achieves its goals. Legislative amendments should be prevented from decreasing effectiveness. Before the legislature makes changes to the insolvency procedure and/or informal restructuring and/or individual recovery procedures, it is important for it to study, or at any rate discuss, their effect on the goals. It is also important to map out what they will cost and to answer the question of who is to bear the costs. The rules should not result in the costs exceeding the benefits. These costs also include the costs of preserving business and employment. All this is essential. Changing an insolvency procedure from the viewpoint of justice without considering the efficiency and effectiveness of the instruments could result in counterproductive legislation.

We can learn from the procedure for the simplified settlement of the insolvency. It is evident from the research that a negligible number of creditors exercise their right to lodge objection against the distribution list in the event of a simplified settlement. It could be said that the benefit of this, a gain in transparency, does not amount to much if we take the number of creditors who object as an indicator. While the costs of the simplified settlement are estimated as high for the creditors: in each simplified settlement, filing costs have to be incurred and it takes the receiver considerable time to go through the compulsory procedure. If we weigh the costs against the benefits, in my opinion such transparency is undesirable. Another example of counterproductive legislation is the amendment of Article 67 (2) of the Bankruptcy Act by the Act of 18 April 2002 for the benefit of employees. I have shown that this amendment does not represent, but actually harms the employees' interests.[19]

Another example of possibly counterproductive future legislation is Articles 3.2.8 and 3.2.9 of the Draft Insolvency Bill. On the basis of these provisions, the receiver is exclusively authorised to file a *Peeters/Gatzen*[20] claim. This is the receiver's authority to claim compensation pursuant to Book 6, Article 162 of the Dutch Civil Code from a third party who cooperated in the prejudicing of creditors by the insolvent, even if the insolvent was not entitled to file such a claim. Under the applicable law, both the individual creditors and the receiver are entitled to do so. It is evident from the research that receivers file claims for prejudicing of creditors in only a small percentage of the insolvencies in which creditors are prejudiced, and that this is successful in an even smaller percentage. The question arises of whether these provisions in the Draft Insolvency Bill will result in counterproductive legislation. The Draft deprives the individual creditors of their right, without making it clear whether the receiver will exercise the right to hold a third party liable. Above all, it is absolutely unknown to what extent there is a convergence in the sense that the receiver and the individual creditors will hold the

---

[19] See A.P.K. Luttikhuis, op. cit. 2007, chapter three.

[20] Named after the so-called Peeters q.q./Gatzen judgment (HR 14 January 1983, NJ 1983, 597).

same third party liable at the same time, and if there is a convergence, to what extent this would affect the goals of the insolvency procedure. Furthermore, the possible positive effect of this right of the individual creditors on the goals of the insolvency procedure remains undiscussed. The advantage of this right of the individual creditors is that if a creditor successfully relies on the third party, that creditor's claim will be (partially) nullified. In that case, the joint creditors would benefit if they received a higher payment and the receiver did not intend to file that claim anyway.

End of the Insolvency Procedure?

The above-mentioned cost-benefit analysis should not be limited to the instruments of the insolvency procedure, but should extend further to the insolvency procedure itself. The legislature and the Dutch Supreme Court can set numerous (social) goals on the insolvency procedure, but the question is who should finance the costs if the estate has no or hardly any assets. The research results show that in three fourths of the corporate insolvencies there was a so-called negative estate and that the size of the companies involved and the number of employees were relatively small.

If the legislature and society consider it desirable that in case there are insufficient assets to pay the receiver's fee, an estate should indeed be settled and social goals pursued, such as, for example combating insolvency fraud, the question arises: in what procedure, by whom and at whose expense? In an insolvency procedure by a receiver at the government's expense, or in another procedure by a government body at the government's expense? If no one wants to bear these costs, it is doubtful whether in a situation in which there are no assets, it would indeed be a matter of course that an insolvency procedure can be pronounced. If there are sufficient assets, it is still not a matter of course that the creditors will finance the costs of the social interests, as I stated in the foregoing.

Chapter 4

Priority Issues in Post-Commencement Financing: A View from South Africa

Kathleen van der Linde

Introduction

The commencement of business rescue or liquidation proceedings has a significant effect on a company's relationship with its existing creditors.[1] It also affects its ability to take up further credit.[2] Yet, post-commencement financing is usually essential to rescuing or reorganising the business or ensuring a better liquidation return to creditors. It may thus be necessary to entice creditors into providing new or further credit by affording them a degree of priority over other creditors.

In this paper I briefly sketch a policy background to the regulation of post-commencement financing and raise a number of practical considerations that I think should be addressed in developing or evaluating a system of regulation. I explore the relevant recommendations of the UNCITRAL Legislative Guide on Insolvency Law.[3] The South African position under the current judicial management system is then analysed and compared to the proposals on business rescue and post-commencement financing under the Companies Bill of 2008,[4] expected to become law in 2010. I set out the position in a winding-up briefly and conclude with a brief evaluation of the South African situation.

---

[1] Their enforcement rights might be suspended by a moratorium or substituted by collective measures. Certain pre-commencement transactions may be set aside under avoidance powers. An insolvency or business rescue practitioner may have the power to suspend or terminate unexecuted contracts. The consequences may differ from jurisdiction to jurisdiction.

[2] In addition to the practical effect on its creditworthiness, the law may prohibit or limit the taking up of further credit.

[3] United Nations Commission on International Trade Law Legislative Guide on Insolvency Law 2005 available at www.uncitral.org/pdf/english/texts/insolven/05-80722_Ebook.pdf (last visited. 30-09-2008) ("UNCITRAL Insolvency Law").

[4] B 61D – 2008, available at www.thedti.gov.za/bills/companies.pdf (last visited 31 December 2008). In preparing this summary I worked with the latest version of the Companies Bill, although it was not yet available at the time of the conference.

Policy considerations

Policy considerations in favour of a priority for post-commencement financing have to be balanced against established principles including the pari passu rule, the vested rights principle, the ideal of upholding commercial bargains and, in regard to secured claims, the prior in tempore maxim.

From the perspective of the providers of post-commencement financing a preference rewards them for the additional risk they assume by extending credit to a financially troubled company rather than to a more creditworthy debtor. The extent to which they may protect themselves through bargaining with the company may be impaired by legal and practical constraints arising from the commencement of the proceedings. If the post-commencement financing has the desired effect of ensuring a better return to pre-commencement creditors, they will have benefited from the risk assumed by the post-commencement creditors. But the pre-commencement creditors bear the risk that the rescue attempt may fail and that they may ultimately receive less than would have been the case under a straightforward liquidation, especially if the preference is continued. Although the prospect of an enhanced return to creditors provides justification for a preference in favour of post-commencement financing, the risk assumed by pre-commencement creditors should be addressed. This can be done by giving them the opportunity of deciding whether they should assume this risk or alternatively by entrusting their protection to a court. The interests of pre-commencement creditors can also be addressed by limiting the preference to instances where it is a necessary incentive to obtaining the post-commencement financing.

The relative bargaining positions of the company and the providers of post-commencement credit is an important normative consideration. New creditors have a free choice whether or not to provide financing. Others, typically existing creditors under ongoing contracts may be obliged to, or have little effective choice but to, continue supplying the company with goods or services on terms that were agreed to on good times. Their position may require a solution different from the one regarded as appropriate for creditors who become involved voluntarily.

The imminent threat of the liquidation alternative with its often negative social and economic impact may justify extraordinary measures aimed at turning around viable businesses. This public interest concern introduces a further dimension to the debate and shifts the focus away from merely resolving the conflict between pre- and post-commencement creditors to the balancing of a broader range of interests.

Practical Considerations

The policy considerations outlined above should be addressed and prioritised in the design or evaluation of a regulatory regime for post-commencement financing. This process may be facilitated by considering the following questions:

- Should priority be given automatically or should it depend on a decision of the existing creditors?
- Which claims should enjoy priority? What kind(s) of priority should be given?
- How should post-commencement creditors rank among themselves?
- Should post-commencement claims of existing creditors under continuing contracts be treated in the same way as creditors providing loans and credit and who become involved out of free choice?
- To what extent should the priority survive bankruptcy proceedings?

The UNCITRAL Legislative Guide on Insolvency Law

The UNCITRAL guide describes the post-commencement financing needs of a debtor and identifies available cash, the sale or realisation of liquid assets, as well as "financing" trough trade credit and loans or other forms of "finance" as possible sources of funding.[5] Incentives for post-commencement financing should be provided where necessary for the continued operation or survival of the business or the preservation or enhancement of the value of the estate.[6] The guide emphasises the need for "new finance" or "new money".[7] A tentative distinction is drawn between financing transactions outside the normal course of business for which a dedicated preference may be necessary[8] and credit or indebtedness incurred in the ordinary course of business which may be treated as administrative expenses.[9] The priority should be established and the only guideline is that it should rank ahead of ordinary unsecured creditors including those unsecured creditors with administrative priority.[10] Priority should survive in an ensuing liquidation, although the ranking may differ from that during business rescue.[11] Court or creditor authorisation for a preference is regarded as optional.[12]

The guide recommends that it should be possible to provide security for post-commencement claims,[13] but that it should not have priority over existing security over that asset without either permission of the security holder or court authorisation.[14] Court authorisation should be subject to giving the security holder the opportunity to be heard; the debtor proving necessity (that it cannot obtain financing in any other way); and protection of interests of security holder (through alternative collateral or periodic payments).[15]

[5] UNCITRAL Insolvency Law, para 94.
[6] UNCITRAL Insolvency Law, recommendation 63.
[7] UNCITRAL Insolvency Law, para 96.
[8] UNCITRAL Insolvency Law, para 104 refers to new "lending" which could be given priority over existing secured creditors, usually subject to proving necessity and protection of existing creditors. Also see par 100.
[9] UNCITRAL Insolvency Law, para 100.
[10] UNCITRAL Insolvency Law, recommendation 64.
[11] See UNCITRAL Insolvency Law, para 107 and recommendation 68.
[12] UNCITRAL Insolvency Law, paras 105-106.
[13] UNCITRAL Insolvency Law, recommendation 65.
[14] UNCITRAL Insolvency Law, recommendation 66.
[15] UNCITRAL Insolvency Law, recommendation 67.

Judicial Management in South Africa

South Africa has a statutory business rescue regime, known as judicial management. A court may grant a judicial management order in respect of a company that is unable or probably unable to pay its debts[16] and has not become a successful concern.[17] The court must be satisfied that there is a reasonable probability that judicial management will enable the company to pay all its debts and become a successful concern.[18] The most significant effect of a judicial management order is that the management of the company is taken over by a judicial manager who has to carry on the company's business, report on its affairs and ensure that it is placed in liquidation if it appears that the company will not be able to pay all its debts and become a successful concern within a reasonable time.[19] The company's assets may not be sold or disposed of otherwise than in the ordinary course of its business or with court authorisation.[20] The court order may impose a moratorium on legal proceedings against the company.[21] The judicial manager does not have the power to terminate existing contracts. A judicial manager may be authorised by the court order to raise money without the authority of the shareholders in any way, but subject to the rights of creditors.[22]

The Act prescribes how the company's assets should be applied during judicial management. Two options are provided, namely a default option[23] and an alternative option that depends on a resolution by the pre-judicial management creditors.[24]

The Default Option

Any monies becoming available to the judicial manager in the course of the judicial management have to be applied "in paying the costs of the judicial management and in the conduct of the company's business in accordance with the judicial management order, and as far as circumstances permit in payment of the claims of pre-judicial management creditors."[25] As far as possible, the costs of judicial management and the claims of creditors must be paid in accordance with

---

[16] Companies Act 1973, s 427(1)(a). In the rest of this paper references to sections are to sections of this Act unless the contrary is indicated.

[17] Section 427(1)(b).

[18] Section 427(1)(b).

[19] Section 433.

[20] Section 434(1).

[21] Section 428(2)(c).

[22] Section 428(2)(c) (provisional order) and s 432(3)(c) (final order). This power is given only if court is absolutely satisfied that creditors and shareholders will be prejudiced if permission is not given, see Standard Bank of South Africa Ltd v Pharmacy Holdings Ltd; Standard Bank of South Africa Ltd v Lennon Ltd 1962 (1) SA 245 (W).

[23] Section 434(2).

[24] Section 435.

[25] Section 434(2).

the position in a sequestration, as if the costs of judicial management were sequestration costs and the claims of creditors were claims in an insolvent estate.[26]

The automatic preference given to administration expenses and post-judicial management claims applies in respect of "monies becoming available" from time to time. Such monies could include cash available upon the appointment of the judicial manager, the proceeds of ordinary trading activities, but also new loans advanced to the company and even the proceeds of assets sold otherwise than in the ordinary course of business.[27]

Pre-judicial management claims should be paid only when circumstances permit, but the circumstances that would permit payment of pre-judicial management creditors are not prescribed. Presumably the intention is that the company's cash flow situation should allow payment of pre-judicial management claims without endangering the payment of expected costs or the continued conduct of the company's business. It is not required that all post-judicial management claims should actually have been settled before pre-judicial management creditors may receive payment. As long as the business can be conducted, even on credit, it would seem that payment may be made to pre-judicial management creditors.

The intervals at which the judicial manager should assess the situation and make payments are not prescribed. This complicates the application of the prescribed ranking to periodic payments, as the claims that could be paid without violating the order of preference may differ depending on the date on which payment is made.

The alternative option

Pre-judicial management creditors may by majority resolution agree to subordinate their claims to all post-judicial management liabilities incurred or to be incurred by the judicial manager in the conduct of the company's business.[28] The post-commencement claims then rank immediately below the costs of judicial management and before all unsecured claims.[29] This preference differs from the default position in several respects. First, the post-commencement liabilities are subject to an internal ranking and enjoy priority in the order in which they were incurred. Secondly, the pre-judicial management unsecured creditors are not entitled to receive payment until all post-judicial management creditors have been paid in full.[30] Thirdly, if the judicial management order is superseded by a

---

[26] Section 434(3). This means that the provisions of the Insolvency Act relating to the ranking of claims, as well as the payment of interest and admission of claims, etc. apply, see Judicial Managers, New Union Goldfields Ltd v New Witwatersrand Gold Exploration Co Ltd 1951 (1) SA 545 (A).

[27] Court permission is required for sales and disposals otherwise than in the ordinary course of the company's business, s 434(1). The proceeds of assets that serve as security must be applied first to pay the secured claim.

[28] Section 435(1)(a).

[29] Section 435(1)(a).

[30] See Ex parte Tasmer NO: In re Angra Enterprises (Pty) Ltd 1957 (1) SA 635 (W) at 639; Chemical Workers Industrial Union and Others v The Master and Another 1997 (2) SA 442 (E) at 447.

winding-up order, the preference continues except that costs of winding-up will also rank ahead of the affected liabilities.[31]

The content of the resolution is circumscribed by section 435(1). As a result, creditors cannot exclude certain liabilities or consent to a different hierarchy.[32] The resolution can be passed at any time during judicial management, even at a meeting where it is decided to end the judicial management and wind up the company.[33] Pre-judicial management creditors who also have post-judicial management claims are not excluded from voting, and so may use their influence in one capacity to their own advantage in the other capacity.

South African courts have interpreted the phrase "liabilities incurred or to be incurred by the judicial manager in the conduct of the company's business" in different ways and the Supreme Court of Appeal has not had the opportunity of clarifying its meaning. In *General Leasing Corporation Ltd v Thorne NO*[34] the court was of the view that the preference was intended primarily for liabilities arising from contracts entered into by the judicial manager in the course of borrowing moneys or acquiring goods or services on credit. Accordingly, liability for damages arising from a judicial manager's decision to breach a pre-judicial management contract did not enjoy a preference in terms of the resolution, despite the fact that the contract was terminated for the purpose of promoting the profitability of the company.[35]

The corresponding provision of the Zimbabwe Companies Act Chap 190 was interpreted in *UDC Ltd v Field NO*[36] when the court had to decide on the ranking of a liability that arose under a post-judicial management guarantee given by the company. The defaulting principal debtor was another company that had taken over a part of the company's indebtedness to a pre-judicial management creditor under a contract of delegation entered into after the commencement of judicial management. The court held that the preference could not be limited to contractual liabilities for loans or credit but extended to any liability incurred for new consideration and which the judicial manager believed was for the benefit of the company.

An even wider interpretation was accepted in *Chemical Workers Industrial Union and Others v The Master and Another.*[37] The dispute related to the ranking of wage claims of employees who had been reinstated by court order following their unfair dismissal. Although the employees had tendered their services as required by the court order, the company and, once the judicial management

---

[31] Section 435(1)(b)(i).
[32] See M.S. Blackman, R.D. Jooste, G.K. Everingham, M. Larkin, C.H. Rademeyer and Y.L. Yeats, Commentary on the Companies Act Looseleaf (2003) Vol 3 at 15-34.
[33] See Ex parte Tasmer NO: In re Angra Enterprises (Pty) Ltd 1957 (1) SA 635 (W) at 636.
[34] 1975 (4) SA 157 (C) at 162-163.
[35] Ibid at 163.
[36] 1980 (4) SA 441 (Z).
[37] 1997 (2) SA 442 (E).

commenced, the provisional and final judicial managers failed to accept the tender of services. The court held that the preference was not restricted to liabilities arising from contracts concluded by the judicial manager but covered all new liabilities, including those which arise out of pre-existing contracts that are continued during judicial management.[38] The court refrained from expressing an opinion on the position of a claim for damages.[39]

The proposed new Business Rescue Procedure for South Africa

Under the Companies Bill[40] which is expected to come into operation in 2010, business rescue proceedings may be commenced either through a resolution of the board of directors[41] or through a court order made on application of shareholders, creditors, a trade union or employees.[42] The company must be in financial distress, meaning that it must face insolvency in either the bankruptcy or equity sense within the ensuing six months.[43] The expected outcome of the proceedings is "rescuing the company" so that it will either continue in existence on a solvent basis or, if this is not possible, yield a better return to creditors or shareholders than if it were to be liquidated immediately.[44] The resolution or court order automatically results in a temporary moratorium[45] and the company is placed under the temporary supervision of a business rescue practitioner.[46] The practitioner may unilaterally cancel or suspend entirely, partially or conditionally any provision of a contract to which the company is a party, except a contract of employment.[47] One of the main duties of the business rescue practitioner is the development and implementation of a business rescue plan.[48] An important advantage in comparison to judicial management is that the plan may provide for a release or discharge of debts.[49]

The Companies Bill expressly allows the company to obtain financing and secure it by utilising company assets to the extent that they are not otherwise encumbered.[50] It provides an automatic preference for post-commencement financing extended during business rescue proceedings. Post-commencement financing will rank in priority to all unsecured claims against the company and subordinate only to the remuneration expenses of the supervisor and other costs of the business rescue proceedings.[51] The preference is continued if liquidation ensues, subject only to the preference in respect of liquidation costs.[52]

[38] Ibid at 448.
[39] Ibid at 448-449.
[40] The new business rescue provisions are set out in Chapter 6 of the Bill. In the rest of this paper references to clauses are to clauses of this Bill.
[41] Clause 129.
[42] Clause 131.
[43] Clause 128(1)(f).
[44] Clause 128(1)(h) read with (b).
[45] Clause 133.
[46] Clause 129(3)(b) (resolution); clause 131(5) (court order).
[47] Clause 136(2). Employees may be retrenched subject to compliance with labour legislation.
[48] Clause 140. The contents of a plan is regulated in clause 150.
[49] Clause 154 read with clause 150(b)(ii).
[50] Clause 135(2).
[51] Clause 135(3).
[52] Clause 135(4).

Any remuneration, reimbursement of expenses or other claim related to employment that becomes due and payable to an employee during business rescue proceedings is regarded as post-commencement financing to the extent that the amount has not been paid to the employee.[53] Employee claims rank equally among themselves, but have preference over all other secured or unsecured post-commencement financing as well as over all other unsecured claims against the company.[54]

Claims in respect of any other post-commencement financing obtained by the company will enjoy preference in the order in which they were incurred over all unsecured claims against the company.[55] The application of this order of preference in a business rescue may cause practical problems. No guidance is provided regarding the timing of and intervals at which payments should be made, but it is clear that the supervisor will have to consider the relative positions and internal ranking of all post-commencement claims each time the company makes a payment. Apparently the company may make payment to employees in the ordinary course of business, as it is only to the extent that an amount has not been paid to an employee that the claim is regarded as post-commencement financing. If wages due to some employees are payable daily or weekly while others are employed on a monthly basis, the equal ranking envisaged in clause 135(3)(a) may exist in theory only.[56]

It is also uncertain whether "claims in respect of" other post-commencement financing refers to instalments that are due and payable, or to the full amount of the indebtedness. If the first interpretation is correct, it is not clear whether the ranking of different claims against the company will be determined by the date on which each instalment is incurred or becomes due or whether the date on which the main debt was incurred will continue to determine the internal ranking of instalments due to different financiers. If the full balance of a financier's claim must be repaid before any payment may be made to a financier who provided financing on a later date, the company will find it difficult to attract financing from different sources.

The preference resembles that which can be granted to post-commencement claims in terms of a resolution under the current Act. In view of the similarity of language it seems that unsecured (pre-commencement) creditors will not be entitled to receive payment until all claims in respect of post-commencement financing have been paid.

The position of secured post-commencement creditors is uncertain, but it would seem that they are entitled to be paid out of general "free residue" funds in accordance with the date that the claim arose. However, if the security is realised, it

---

[53] Clause 135(1)(a).
[54] Clause 135(3)(a). An earlier version of the Bill provided that employee claims would rank in the order in which they were incurred.
[55] Clause 135(3)(b).
[56] The monthly claims of employees may rank equally with the weekly claims of employees who have already received payment for 3 of the 4 weeks in that month. The employees with monthly claims will thus be in a worse position than those with weekly claims, especially if the majority of employees have weekly claims.

can be assumed that the secured claims will be paid from the proceeds of the security to the extent that it has not been applied in respect of the super-preferent claims of employees. Any balance remaining will rank with the unsecured claims according to the date on which the claim arose.

The concept "financing obtained"[57] appears to be narrower in scope than "liabilities incurred". I think it presupposes an agreement between the creditor and the company in terms of which funds are supplied or goods and services provided on credit. As the preference applies to financing "obtained" during business rescue proceedings, an argument can be made for the inclusion of the supply of further funds or the provision of further goods and services on credit under a pre-existing contract.

The business rescue plan must set out the order of preference in which the "proceeds of property" will be applied to pay creditors.[58] Although there is room for doubt, it would seem that the plan cannot change the order of preference in respect of creditors providing post-commencement financing.[59]

Post-Liquidation Financing in South Africa

The South African position in respect of post-liquidation financing is regulated by separate provisions which differ from the business rescue scenario in several respects. No provision is made for priority in respect of post-commencement financing, but certain expenses may be regarded as part of the costs of the winding-up and so enjoy preferential treatment. It would seem that providers of such post-liquidation financing will be better off than post-judicial management creditors, because of the wider definition of costs of winding-up which includes costs of conducting the business.

For the time being, the liquidation proceedings of the current Companies Act will continue to apply until the enactment of a unified Bankruptcy Act.[60] The inconsistent treatment of post-business rescue financing and post-liquidation financing will remain.

Evaluation and Conclusion

Although the South African provisions comply in broad outline with the recommendations of the UNCITRAL guide, they remain subject to criticism. The current and proposed provisions on post-commencement financing are in my view

---

[57] Clause 135(2).

[58] Clause 150(2)((b)(v). The plan must also identify the property of the company that is to be available to pay creditors' claims, clause 150(2)(b)(iv).

[59] In view of the policy of strong protection of employee rights in South Africa, it is unlikely that the legislature would allow creditors in general to determine a different ranking for post-commencement employee claims. Since the plan has to compare the position of creditors in a liquidation and under business rescue (clause 150(2)(b)(vi), an inference that this clause is restricted to pre-commencement creditors is justified. The reference to proceeds of property rather than to income in general supports this deduction. However, this interpretation does not address the position of post-commencement claims otherwise than in respect of financing.

[60] Companies Bill, schedule 5 item 9.

too rigid. A resolution under section 435 includes all liabilities incurred by the judicial manager after commencement. Similarly, under the Bill all "financing" will automatically enjoy preference. The order of preference among different post-commencement claims is pre-determined by the date on which each claim arose and may be difficult to apply in practice. The uncertainty regarding which liabilities qualify under the preference also complicates matters.

This rigidity may inhibit the realisation of the primary objective of conferring priority on post-commencement financing, namely to facilitate and provide incentives for financing, as no distinction is made between different claims on the basis of the expected contribution they will make, or the necessity of providing an incentive in respect of the particular transaction. There is no room for a hierarchy between claims regarded as more deserving of priority.

I regard the absence of an authorisation requirement in the proposed new procedure is a deficiency. While an automatic preference could be justified on public policy grounds if there is a high likelihood of preserving the company, it may be unfair to force existing creditors to bear the risk imposed by the preference in instances where the only potential benefit they could possibly obtain is a marginally return compared to immediate liquidation.

The differences in the treatment of post-judicial management and post-liquidation financing, particularly in relation to post-commencement liabilities arising from continuing pre-existing contracts are difficult to justify. I suggest that greater coherence in the treatment of post-commencement claims during business rescue and liquidation is desirable.

Chapter 5

Bankruptcy Law Reform in China: Achievements and Challenges

Zhang Xian-Chu

Introduction

The long-awaited new Enterprise Bankruptcy Law of the People's Republic China ("PRC") was finally adopted on 27 August 2006 by the Standing Committee of the National People's Congress (the "new Law") as the result of the unremitting legislative efforts of twelve years and has come into force on 1 June 2007. The new enactment has received general welcome from the commentators for its innovative and reform measures to modernize China's bankruptcy legal regime.[1]

Development of Bankruptcy Law and Practice in China

The State-Owned Enterprise Bankruptcy Law (the "SOE Bankruptcy Law") as the first bankruptcy legislation in the PRC history was adopted in 1986 with only 43 short and general articles. The historical legislation was considered a milestone of the economic reform and an important breakthrough of the political ideology in a socialist country like China where bankruptcy as a market institution had not been heard since 1949 in the planned economy.

The enactment, however, was highly controversial due to its political implications on the sensitive public ownership and as a result, adopted merely on a trial basis. Moreover, the SOE Bankruptcy Law suffered from some congenital deficiencies. Among them, two concerns are the most fundamental: underdeveloped social welfare system in China to support bankruptcy enforcement and lack of a uniform legal regime in enterprise bankruptcy practice.

The aggressive SOE reform has made 36 million workers laid off in 1995 -2002;[2] 12-13 million new labourers enter into the market every year since 2002 and rural labour surplus has been estimated to have reached 150 million.[3] The

---

[1] Wang Pei, "Bankruptcy Legislation Passed", China International Business, Nov. 2006, at 26; and Eu Jin, "China's New Bankruptcy Law: A Legislative Innovation", China Law & Practice, Oct. 2006, at 17-20.

[2] J. Giles, A. Park and Juwei Zhang, "What is China's True Unemployment Rate?", 16 China Economic Review (2005), at 150.

[3] Kyodo, "China Faces Worst Unemployment Problem in 4 Years", Asian Economic News, May 6, 2002; available at www.finarticle.com/p/articles/mi_m0WDP/is_2002_May_6/ai_85519929.

substantially increased unemployment has been one of the biggest challenges to the government to maintain the economic development and the social stability of China.

Moreover, the potential financial crisis has been another crucial factor in bankruptcy practice in China. The massive bankruptcy of SOEs would inevitably mean the bankruptcy of the state owned banks as SOE's capital suppliers. As such, the practice that subjects SOE bankruptcy to the state plan and policy with the bankruptcy quota and workers' settlement priority has been developed since the 1990s in order to deal with the huge amount of non-performing loan problems. Worse yet, the defective infrastructure has fuelled rampant bankruptcy frauds by way of unlawful transfer of debtors' assets and false transformation of SOEs. According to an official report of the People's Bank of China, SOE bankruptcy fraud cases made 69.37 per cent of all the fraudulent violations in the country concerning SOEs and state assets.[4]

The other fundamental problem of the bankruptcy regime in China has been the lack of a uniform law applicable to all the market players. The SOE Bankruptcy Law was applicable only to state owned enterprises whereas the Civil Procedure Law of 1991 and the Company Law of 1993 also set out different rules applicable to bankruptcy of other types of enterprises. In order to deal with practical problems, numerous judicial interpretations and provisions have been promulgated by the Supreme People's Court as well as many local courts. This situation forms an uneven level playing field and leads to chaotic judicial practices. As such, the development of bankruptcy law in China has been challenged by not only the political ideology and administrative intervention, but also the developing market institutional conditions and the defective legislation itself.

The Bankruptcy Law Reform in 2007

The new Law, which includes 136 articles in 12 chapters, introduces reform measures in almost all the aspects and quite a few new institutions:

A New Uniform Bankruptcy Test

The new Law will apply to enterprises of all kinds with legal person status. Article 2 unifies the bankruptcy standard with a new two-tier insolvency test. It stipulates that an enterprise shall enter into the liquidation proceeding if:

- it is unable to repay the debt due; and
- its assets prove insufficient to pay off all the debts or it apparently lacks capability to repay its debts. This test obviously intends to leave some discretion on the hand of the People's Court in dealing with insolvency cases.

---

[4] The Report of the People's Bank of China on Enterprise Schemes to Evade Financial Obligations dated March 16, 2001, printed at The Bulletin of the State Council of PRC, no. 18 (2001), at 12-15 (in Chinese).

The Intersection of Insolvency and Company Laws

The Mechanism of Bankruptcy Administrators

The new Law empowers the People's Court, once a bankruptcy case is accepted, to appoint an administrator to replace the government led liquidation group under the old law. A bankruptcy administrator has a wide range of powers as well as the duty of due diligence and faithfulness subject to the supervision of the People's Court and the creditors' meeting.

A Reorganization System

Chapter 8 of the new Law introduces an American style reorganization regime to reform the consolidation mechanism under the government control under the SOE Bankruptcy Law, which would only commence after the bankruptcy proceeding. As a result, the parties may initiate early rescue in order to avoid bankruptcy of the debtor.

Under the new Law, the debtor enterprise or the administrators shall submit their reorganization plan to the People's Court and the creditors' meeting within six months of the court's ruling for the reorganization. The reorganization plan, once put forward, shall be voted by different creditors' groups respectively. Such a plan shall be adopted if the creditors of all the categories vote for it. If the reorganization plan fails to be approved by certain category of creditors, another vote may be carried out after the consultation between the debtor or the administrators and the dissenting creditors concerned. Where the plan is voted down again, the People's Court may approve the plan by "cramming down" the creditors' opposition based on the petition of the debtor or the administrator within 30 days as long as it satisfies certain legal and feasible conditions on fair compensation and repayment.

Once the reorganization plan is approved by the People's Court, the debtor may manage its own assets and carry out its business operation under the supervision of the administrator and the People's Court. As a result, the concept of "debtor in possession" is officially recognized in the new Law and bankruptcy practice in China.

In addition to reorganization, the new Law also allows unsecured creditors to reach settlement with the debtor enterprise before the bankruptcy declaration through the debtor's petition to the People's Court and approval of the majority creditors who are present at the creditors' meeting and represent two third of unsecured claims.

Improvements to the Bankruptcy Regime

Improvements have come in this area with more detailed rules that incorporate the judicial practice developed in the past twenty years and are borrowed from the experiences of the developed economies. For example, a creditors' committee is stipulated in the new Law to facilitate the progress of judicial proceedings in an efficient way in large bankruptcy cases; the bankruptcy expenses and debts in common benefit are dealt with in a specific chapter; and more sophisticated recovery rules with different chase-back periods in the bankruptcy proceedings are developed. Moreover, certain claims to recover the assets transferred before the commencement of the bankruptcy proceeding can be exercised within two years of the completion of the distribution under the new Law, instead of one year under the old law. The changes clearly intend to provide creditors with more protection against fraudulent bankruptcy. The new Law also sets out rules governing automatic stay, set-off, and directors' fiduciary duty during the bankruptcy proceedings.

Enhancement of Employee Protection in Bankruptcy Proceedings

Despite being a big controversy during the legislative process, the new Law sets out rules to provide workers of bankrupt enterprises with more legal protections. As a general principle, Article 6 requires the People's Court in bankruptcy trials to safeguard the workers' lawful rights and interests in accordance with the law.

Moreover, claims of the employees for their unpaid pension contribution, social insurances and other compensations need not be registered with the People's Court. Bankruptcy administrators shall carry out their investigation, make a detailed list and make it known to the workers concerned. All these payments in arrears enjoy their priority in bankruptcy distribution over the state taxation and claims of general creditors. Moreover, the creditors' meeting shall include the representatives of employees or the trade union.

Setting out a Cross-Border Insolvency Provision

Article 5 of the new Law states that a domestic bankruptcy proceeding shall have its legal effects on the assets of the debtor enterprise concerned outside the territory of China. A foreign bankruptcy judgment or ruling concerning the assets of the debtor in China may be recognized and enforced on the basis of international treaty or agreement or the reciprocity principle if it does not violate the basic principles of the Chinese law, social public interests of China, and "the lawful interests of creditors within the territory of China". Although the single provision of the new Law apparently lacks of the necessary details, it does reflect the ideological progress made in recent years and the government's more willingness to close the gap with the practice of most developed economies according to the universal principle.

Implementation of the New Law

Since the adoption of the new Law, many new national laws and administrative regulations have set up their connections with it, including the Law of Agricultural Cooperatives, the Labour Contract Law and the Property Law.

In order to implement the new Law, some judicial interpretations have been issued. In April 2007, the Supreme People's Court promulgated two circulars governing appointment of bankruptcy administrators and their remuneration. The High People's Courts at the provincial level shall adopt the professional administrators' list within their own jurisdictions. The selection shall be made by an assessment committee of the People's Court concerned according to the competence, service record, professional performance and experience of the candidates.[5] Although the circulars do not specify whether foreign firms and practitioners may be appointed bankruptcy administrators, their participation should not be ruled out. In fact foreign firms have been appointed in the high profile bankruptcy liquidation of Guangdong International Trust and Investment Company (GITIC) since 1999 and such practice is considered to have improved transparency and impartiality of the bankruptcy procedures.

A bankruptcy administrator shall be paid on a progressive basis according to the total property value finally distributed. However, the High People's Courts may formulate the ranges applicable to their own jurisdictions according to the local conditions and have the power to further adjust the remuneration according to the concrete conditions of a given case and the performance of the administrator.

Unsettled Issues and Further Concerns

There is no doubt that the new Law modernizes the bankruptcy regime in China in many aspects; however, the new enactment does not solve all the problems.

Continuation of the Dual-Track System in the Transitional Period

Despite the uniform system to be established in the future, Article 133 of the new Law provides that the state policy applicable to SOE bankruptcy before the adoption of the new Law may still be applied within the term and scope stipulated by the State Council. As such, the policy bankruptcy and the bankruptcy proceedings under the new Law will exist side by side in practice after the new Law enters into force. Although the Central Government has promised to end the policy bankruptcy by 2009, given more than two thousands of SOEs remaining on the list of the policy bankruptcy arrangements concerning 3.51 million workers and unpaid debts to the state banks of RMB 227.16 billion,[6] the job may not be done on time.

---

[5] Art. 7 of the Provision.

[6] Opinions of the National Leading Group on Further Carrying Out Closing-down and Bankruptcy of State Owned Enterprises under the State Policy of 16 January 2006 endorsed by the State Council.

Moreover, such policy bankruptcy practice may even be expanded to bankruptcy of non-SOE enterprises in the transitional period. Article 132 stipulatesthat after the implementation of the new Law, if the workers' wages, medical expenses, injury or disability allowance, pension and other social insurance payments, or other compensations required by the law or regulations were in arrear before 26 August 2006 as the promulgation day of the Law, the unpaid sum shall enjoy a special treatment, regardless the type of the bankrupt enterprise concerned. If the sum cannot get paid in full according to the normal distribution order subordinate to the secured interests, the unpaid part shall take the priority as secured claims to receive distribution.

Failure to introduce Personal Bankruptcy

In the long course of drafting, whether individual bankruptcy should be included was heatedly debated. In China the consumers market is rapidly developing. In addition, a large number of individuals have engaged in business in forms of individual commercial households, partnership enterprises, sole proprietorship enterprises, and other business forms based on individuals' liability. Against this background, personal bankruptcy rules are urgently needed. As matter of fact, some rules in this regard were included in the draft that was submitted to the national legislature for the first reading, but deleted since the second reading. As a result, the new Law is called "a half bankruptcy law".[7]

Continued Legal Vacuum on the Bankruptcy of Financial Institutions

Lack of legal rules governing financial institutional bankruptcy has troubled the People's Courts in many legal proceedings dealing with bankruptcy of financial institutions, including commercial banks, investment companies and securities firms. Mr. Zhou Xiaochuan, the Governor of the People's Bank of China expressed his high hope in the course of drafting for the new bankruptcy law to provide its strong institutional support with the financial reform in China.[8]

Despite the strong needs and desires, the new Law finally gave up its attempt to include a special chapter to deal with bankruptcy of financial institutions. Art. 134 merely states that the state banking regulatory authority may petition to the People's Court for reorganization or bankruptcy of financial institutions. If the state authority has taken measures to take over or take custody of a financial institution concerned in order to deal with significant operational risks, the People's Court upon the state authority's application may stay any creditor's enforcement proceeding. However, the legal rules governing financial institution bankruptcy shall be adopted by the State Council in a later time.

[7] See Duan Hongqing, "Promulgation of the New Bankruptcy Law", Financial Magazine, 166 (2006), available at caijing.hexun.com/text.aspx?sl=2304&id=1789497 (in Chinese).
[8] See the report of Financial Times, December 3, 2004 (in Chinese).

Worries have been raised with the qualification and competence of the judiciary to deal with challenges in application and enforcement of the new rules, which will require not only good understanding of the law and skilful handling cases, but also professional understanding of their potential implications to all the parties and the feasibility of reorganization schemes, settlement proposals, distribution plans and suggestions of business continuation. As such, the People's Court will, together with the new Law, be tested in the practice on "whether the law will be applied fairly and consistently" and whether there are adequately trained judges and professionals to implement this complex legislation.[9]

A more fundamental concern is on judicial integrity and impartiality, including commanding professional conduct and resisting unlawful intervention from the government by the judges.[10] Almost immediately after the adoption of the new Law, a big corruption case with RMB multi-millions involving several senior judges including a vice president of the Shenzhen Intermediate People's Court, in a bankruptcy case was widely reported where a biased and fraudulent decision was found against foreign parties.[11] The shocking incident with a series of arrests also led to revealing of more bankruptcy scandals. In this context, it seems clear that the bankruptcy law regime cannot be upgraded in isolation, but to be developed with the entire infrastructure and environment of the country.

Conclusion

The bankruptcy law reform is a positive sign of the serious commitment of China to a market economy and the rule of law. The enactment and implementation of the new Law will mark a new era of bankruptcy practice with a higher degree of adaptation to the international practice and an accelerated evolution of bankruptcy regime and culture in China.

In line with the new reorientation, the government-led closure is being replaced with a more judicial controlled process. The new Law codified the expansion of the judicial powers in supervising the entire bankruptcy proceedings, adjudicating disputes among all the parties, making final decisions on reorganization, bankruptcy declaration, distribution, avoidance claims and other crucial matters, and imposing liabilities. At the same time, it will enable market professionals to play more active roles in bankruptcy administration, reorganization and workout, liquidation, distribution, and recovery of assets.

Despite the notable progress and modernization, there is still much room for the new regime to further improve itself. Some serious challenges remain and will continue to test the government's willingness to respect the market discipline and the judicial competence to effectively implement the law.

[9] J.J. Rapisardi and D.A. Palmer, "China's New Bankruptcy Law: Doing Business in China", New York Law Journal, October 20, 2006.
[10] Eu, supra note 1, at 20.
[11] For a brief report, see Chow Chung-Yan, "Probe into Shenzhen Judiciary Escalates", South China Morning Post, October 27, 2006, at 4.

PART II
SPECIAL BRIEFING

Chapter 6

The ALI-III Project on Global Principles in International Insolvency

Bob Wessels

Introduction

The American Law Institute ("ALI") is a renowned organisation, established in 1923 by judges, legal practitioners and academics. ALI's general aim is "to promote the clarification and simplification of the law and to secure the better administration of justice". Outside the USA, ALI is known mainly for its role in the realization of so-called Restatements, which are comprehensive descriptions and explanations of certain major topics of law, such as the Restatements on the Law of Agency or on Contracts.[1] In 2000, the ALI approved a set of principles, called "Principles of Cooperation in Transnational Insolvency Cases Among the Members of the North American Free Trade Agreement". These "Principles" comprise 7 "General Principles", 27 "Procedural Principles" and 7 "Recommendations for Legislation or International Agreement". The architect of the Principles is Professor Jay Westbrook.

Added to these Principles is an Appendix B, with the title: "Guidelines Applicable to Court-to-Court Communications in Cross-Border Cases".[2] These Guidelines (17 in all) in general codify experiences and practice resulting from some fifteen cross-border cases in which courts in different jurisdictions have mutually aligned their approaches, their communication, their supervision and their completion of a cross-border insolvency case (whether based on a Protocol or not). The Guidelines have been translated into some fifteen languages, mainly as an effort by individual members of the International Insolvency Institute ("III").[3]

---

[1] For an overview, see M. Traynor, "The First Restatements and the Vision of the American Law Institute, Then and Now", in: 32 Southern Illinois University Law Journal 2007, 145. For a critical analysis of the influence of the ALI's Restatements on the development of United States common law, see K. Adams, "The Folly of Uniformity. Lessons from the Restatement Movement", in: 33 Hofstra Law Review 2004, 423ff. For an overview of ALI's currents projects, see www.ali.org/index.cfm?fuseaction = projects.currentprojects.

[2] See: J. Westbrook (reporter), International Statement of United States Bankruptcy Law (2nd volume in: American Law Institute, Transnational Insolvency: Cooperation Among the NAFTA Countries, 4 Volumes), JP Juris Publishing, Inc., 2003.

[3] These non-authorized translations can be found at www.iiiglobal.org. See J. Westbrook, "The Transnational Insolvency Project of the American Law Institute", in: 17 Connecticut Journal of International Law 2001, 99, and J. Westbrook, "Multinational Enterprises in General Default: Chapter

Judges in Canada and the USA have applied the Guidelines in several cases, some of them I have analysed in earlier publications.[4]

The Guidelines relate to the Principles of Cooperation in Transnational Insolvency Cases Among the Members of the North American Free Trade Agreement, specifically Procedural Principle 10 ("Communications"):

> "To the maximum extent permitted by domestic law, courts considering bankruptcy proceedings or requests for assistance from foreign bankruptcy courts should communicate with each other directly or through administrators. To the maximum extent, such communications should take advantage of modern methods of communication including telephone, telefacsimile, teleconferencing, and electronic mail, as well as written documents delivered in traditional ways. Any such communications should at all times follow procedures consistent with domestic law as to such matters."

The Principle was adopted by unanimity among the experts involved in drafting of these ALI Principles.[5] It has met its equal in Articles 25–27 in Chapter IV ("Cooperation with foreign courts and foreign representatives") UNCITRAL Model Law, which encapsulates a more broad scope by also including the desirability of cross-border communication and cooperation between courts and foreign representatives.

A growing group of countries have introduced or amended their legal system concerning in ternational insolvency law inspired by the UNCITRAL Model Law. In 2008, eleven years after the publication of the Model Law, the following countries have, to a varying extent, enacted the Model Law into domestic law: Australia (2008),[6] British Virgin Islands (2005), Colombia (2006), Eritrea (2000), Great Britain (2006), Japan (2000), Mexico (2000), Montenegro (2002), New Zealand (2006), Poland (2003), Republic of Korea (2006), Romania (2003), Serbia (2004), South-Africa (2000) and the USA (2005).[7] In some countries, legislative proposals have been suggested or have been debated within the legislative forum (the country's parliament), examples of such countries are Argentina, the Cayman Islands, Canada, Pakistan[8] and, in November 2007, the Netherlands.

15, the ALI Principles, and the EU Insolvency Regulation", in: 76 American Bankruptcy Law Journal 2002, 30ff.

[4] See B. Wessels, "Nederlands insolventierecht internationaliseert", in: Weekblad voor Privaatrecht, Notariaat en Registratie (WPNR) 6456 (2001); B. Wessels, "Internationaal insolventierecht als motor van grensoverschrijdende coördinatie en samenwerking tussen rechters en curatoren", in: Tijdschrift voor Insolventierecht (TvI) 2002, 21; B. Wessels, International Insolvency Law, 2nd ed., 2006, para. 10115ff. For most of these cases, see www.iiiglobal.org.

[5] J. Westbrook (reporter), International Statement of United States Bankruptcy Law (2nd volume in: American Law Institute, Transnational Insolvency: Cooperation Among the NAFTA Countries, 4 Volumes), JP Juris Publishing, Inc., 2003, 57.

[6] The Cross-Border Insolvency Act 2008 (Cth) received royal assent on 26 May 2008 and are scheduled to come into effect on 26 November 2008.

[7] See www.uncitral.org, UNIS/L/118, 21 May 2008.

[8] See B. Wessels, "Will Uncitral Bring Changes to Insolvency Proceedings Outside the USA and Great Britain? It certainly will!", Paper presented during 4th European Corporate Restructuring Summit, 26 and 27 April 2006, London, available via: www.bobwessels.nl/uk/recente_artikelen.php and: UNCITRAL Note by the Secretariat "Insolvency law: Developments in insolvency law: adoption of the UNCITRAL Model Law on Cross-Border Insolvency; use of the cross-border protocols and court-to-court communication guidelines; and case law on

Towards Global Rules

In this heavily changed environment, further discussed below, it is challenging to meet the goal of the project referred to in the title of this publication. The project is led by Professor Ian Fletcher, University College of London, and myself, both being appointed as Reporters by ALI. The goal of the project is to establish the extent to which it is feasible to achieve a worldwide acceptance of the NAFTA Principles together with the Guidelines, either in their existing form or, if necessary, with modifications or variations. In assessing the reactions to the Questionnaires the Reporters have set out regarding the Principles, it is submitted that two clear lines of reasoning can be detected. Firstly, the explanation given to ALI Procedural Principle 10 and the objections articulated against court-to-court communication still hold to a great extend. Secondly, the degree of global consensus that has emerged from the questionnaires is significant. Outside the NAFTA jurisdictions there is only a handful of jurisdiction that largely covers the contents of the Guidelines, but – besides legal obstacles – there is generally large support for the core of the Guidelines, although it is noted (as will be discussed below) that the professional quality of the logistics of organizations such as courts is a candidate for improvement and language barriers are seen as significant challenges to be overcome.

Furthermore, it is striking to see the pace the developments regarding the topic of cross-border communication between courts has taken during the last ten years. Generally speaking, one ALI Procedural Principle (Principle 10) in conjunction with Articles 25–27 of the UNCITRAL Model Law, presently is mirrored in some 15 countries. In Europe, in all Member States (except for Denmark), Article 31 of the EC Insolvency Regulation introduced in 2002 cross-border communication and cooperation between insolvency office holders (not being courts). In all the landscape of international insolvency law has changed dramatically since the issuance of said Guidelines Applicable to Court-to-Court Communications in Cross-Border Cases ("Guidelines").

Communication and coordination of cross-border insolvency cases, either by courts and/or insolvency office holders, now is clearly the paradigm in solving questions in cross-border insolvency matters. Communication and cooperation has emerged as the driving force in the area of methods or principles which have been debated since time immemorial, with in it most extreme forms the principles of universality and territoriality. These latter notions fight a rearguard action, where mitigated and mixed forms of these methods have gained there presence in many insolvency legislations all over the world, to which the procedural paradigm of communication and cooperation has been or is added which interconnects the legal systems of jurisdictions involved. Cross-border court-to-court coordination of specific cases, developed by many insolvency practitioners since the beginning of

interpretation of "centre of main interest" and "establishment" in the European Union" (Doc. A/CN.9/580 (14 April 2005)). See also I.R.C. Kawaley, "Judicial co-operation in cross-border insolvency cases: recent offshore developments", in: 20 Insolvency Intelligence, September/October 2007, 113ff.

the 1980s and supported by such institutes as UNCITRAL, the World Bank, ALI and III, are now the benchmark for the present generation.

Insofar as the matters regulated in Articles 25–27 did not already exist in domestic law, they have been taken into account by those jurisdictions which have introduced or amended their legal system concerning international insolvency law, inspired by the UNCITRAL Model Law. As a result, in 2008, the following countries have adopted rules concerning communication and cooperation in cross-border cases: Mexico, USA, UK, Poland, Romania and, a few months ago, Australia. Other countries adopting this concept include Slovenia and South Africa, which has adopted the UNCITRAL Model Law (enacted as the Cross-Border Insolvency Act 42 of 2000 in South Africa) that allows for coordination and cooperation between courts. The Act itself is not in operation because of its designation/reciprocity clause that calls for the Minister of Justice to designate countries to which the Act would apply. Unfortunately, the Minister has not yet designated any such countries. Not (directly) related to the Model Law, but inspired by other examples, also in other countries rules regarding cross-border communication and cooperation have been adopted. Examples include Germany, Belgium, Croatia, Spain and Vietnam.

Provisions regarding Cross-Border Cooperation in Germany, Belgium and Spain

The German law imposes a clear mandate for cooperation between domestic and foreign insolvency administrators. A domestic administrator must cooperate fully with a foreign counterpart, including communicating immediately any information which may be relevant for the realization of the foreign proceedings and allowing the foreign administrator to attend creditor's meetings. The foreign administrator must receive an opportunity to submit proposals for the liquidation or use of German assets and, if a restructuring plan is being developed, to comment on the plan. The foreign administrator is also entitled to submit his or her own plan.[9] If all domestic creditors in a secondary proceeding can be paid in full using the proceeds of assets in Germany, the domestic administrator is required to turn over any surplus to the foreign administrator of main proceedings.[10]

In 2004, of particular interest is the provision in Belgium entitled "Duty to Inform and Cooperate."[11] It reads as follows:

"The liquidator of principal proceedings or territorial proceedings opened by a court having jurisdiction on the basis of article 118 §1 part 2 is duty bound to cooperate and communicate information with the liquidators of foreign insolvency proceedings concerning the debtor. This

[9] Id. § 357.
[10] Id. § 358.
[11] Id. Art. 120.

duty applies only if the law of the state where the proceedings were opened provides on a reciprocal basis for an equivalent cooperation and communication duty in respect of the relevant proceedings. The duties described in the preceding part are to be fulfilled insofar as the costs of registration, publicity and cooperation are not unreasonable, taking into account the assets of the estate, even if the law of the foreign state would legally require some local measures. If the liquidation of the estate of territorial proceedings offers the possibility to satisfy all admitted claims in full, the liquidator appointed in these proceedings will transfer the balance immediately to the liquidator of the principal proceedings, on condition of a reciprocal co-operation and communication duty in the relevant proceedings."

The provision therefore creates a conditional duty and only applies on a reciprocal basis. It is noteworthy that the present system in Belgium is regarded as limiting the country's previous position, in that it applied the principle of universality "in a radical and unwavering way."[12]

In Spain, Article 227 of the Ley Concursal imposes on insolvency organs the obligation to cooperate with foreign insolvency proceedings. The provision includes the exchange of information, the coordination of the administration and control of the insolvent's estate, and the approval and application by the courts of agreements related to coordination of the proceedings.

Obstacles to Cross-Border Cooperation

Presently, in some forty jurisdictions, certain forms of communication and coordination of cross-border insolvency cases, either by courts and/or insolvency office holders have been introduced:
- in law, as "best practice" guidelines or a combination of the two; or
- with global application or within geographical limited regions (Europe); or
- limited to communication and cooperation between insolvency office holders (Europe) or including courts (in Europe for relations with non-Member States, e.g. in legislation in Belgium, Croatia, England and Wales, Germany, Poland, Slovenia, Spain, and draft legislation in the Netherlands).

Although the legal framework and practical reality of many countries will hinder the application of the Guidelines, it is noted that there is generally large support for the core of the Guidelines.

The main hindrances to applying the Guidelines in the way as has been demonstrated in USA and Canada are of five kinds:
- existing law;
- role of the court;
- reciprocity;
- language; and
- legal terminology.

The latter two are of a more general nature and not specifically related to matters of insolvency. Some remarks regarding the first three follow below.

---

[12] See P. Torremans, Cross Border Insolvencies in EU, English and Belgian Law, European Monographs no. 39, at 12 (2002).

In a large group of countries, the law, including its constitution and its procedural statutes, determine strictly the powers of a court and the practical procedural actions a court is allowed to take. In their interpretations or decisions courts may be guided by the rationale of certain of the Guidelines, but they lack the authority to "adopt" or "apply" the Guidelines and/or to suggest to another court to "approve" the suggested course of dealing with the specific cross-border insolvency case, or conversely to "approve" certain approaches suggested by a foreign court. Any breach of domestic rules of such nature, laid down in a judgment of a court of first instance, is subject to nullification. In such circumstances any effort to introduce measures based on effectiveness or practical common sense, also when these measures are for the best of the debtor and the creditors concerned, run the risk of nullification. In the end in such a jurisdiction it may ultimately be counterproductive to follow an approach based on the "application" of certain Guidelines, as it will generally lead to no result and will be time consuming too. In other countries the rules regarding communication or cooperation may be regarded as limited or with insufficient clarity.

The Guidelines assume an active role for the courts involved. In certain countries a court may have a different role, i.e. only acting after having been explicitly requested by the debtor, the insolvency office holder, by a creditor or by any other interested party, which is allowed to do so either based on the law of the courts' jurisdiction or the rules applicable in a cross-border insolvency case. The mutuality of court-to-court communication as assumed by the Guidelines (communications "to the maximum extend" possible) is based on the rationale that courts on an equal footing work together towards a common goal. Both courts have an equal interest to know all relevant details of the case to be able to arrange for providing solutions to problems which arise between the proceedings. Where the applicable law does not allow a court (fully) to collect facts or evidence, communication or cooperation with another court is due to fail.

In the area of international insolvency, a much wider concept will hinder the application of the ALI Guidelines and the Court-to-Court Guidelines. It is the concept of sovereignty insofar as it serves to protect a State's general economic and social policies or its existing judicial framework. An illustration of its wider impact relates to the UNCITRAL Model Law. Although rejected as an approach during the negotiations of the Model Law, a number of countries have adopted provisions applying the Model Law on a reciprocal basis, although the nature of these reciprocity provisions varies: Argentina (draft), British Virgin Islands, Canada (draft), Mexico, Romania and South Africa. Unrelated to the Model Law, Belgium, China, Jersey and Spain and Tanzania apply reciprocity provisions.

An Independent Intermediary?

What would be a solid way to go forward? The views expressed here are my personal ones which, moreover, must be regarded as rather tentative. Article 27 of the UNCITRAL Model Law provides for an unlimited variety of methods to facilitate cross-border cooperation:
- appointment of a person or body to act at the direction of the court;
- communication of information by any means considered appropriate by the court;
- coordination of the administration and supervision of the debtor's assets and affairs;
- approval or implementation by courts of agreements concerning the coordination of proceedings;
- coordination of concurrent proceedings regarding the same debtor;
- any additional forms or examples of cooperation the enacting State may wish to list.[13]

I suggest the further expansion of Article 27(a) (Appointment of a person or body to act at the direction of the court) with the appointment of an officer, provisionally called: "independent intermediary". [14]Such an official could operate as an alternative to or as an addition to court-to-court communication, directly or through administrators, and the cooperation by way of a "protocol". A first draft of a provisional principle, with the heading "Intermediary", [15]could be the following:

"1. A court is advised to consider, in its own right or at the request of any administrator or any creditor, whether the appointment of an independent intermediary would better ensure coordination between different proceedings under the courts' supervision.
2. The function of an intermediary is to help ensure that a transnational insolvency proceeding is operated in accordance with the goals of the Global Principles, the provisions set in a protocol or provision contained in the court's decision.
3. The court should solicit the views of the administrators in each of the pending insolvency proceedings prior to such an appointment.
4. An intermediary will be a person with good ability and intelligence, experience, professional knowledge, good character, acting impartial and avoiding the perception of possible conflict of interest.
5. An intermediary is accountable to the court.
6. The court may award intermediary's fees and costs out of the estate of the insolvency proceeding in which it has jurisdiction."

As it presently stands, at the international level, there is to a large extent agreement as to the role a court could play in cross-border insolvency cases and the principles that would apply to such cases. As explained earlier, practical and legal obstacles hinder the realisation of the exercise of a court's responsibilities. How to remove these obstacles? The practical obstacles may be by-passed with the

---

[13] The Guide to Enactment (1997), nr. 183, only gives an explanation for category (f).
[14] For other suggestions I refer to my inaugural lecture, footnote 1 above.
[15] Also another possible name, such as "monitor", comes to mind if this official also is assigned with coordination, has certain rights to push matters forward, and can signal in its own right problems to the court.

alternative presented above. A court may wish to decline from communication with another foreign court or through administrators for reasons such as the case-load pending, the perceived complexity of a certain cross-border case, including the variety of stakeholders, the unavailability of (e-)technological means, the problems that may be foreseen with multi-lingual communications or the perceived conflicts between administrators. Moreover, also for sound reasons of maintaining impartiality, a court may wish to stay away from direct communications or assign these to an administrator, who will have his/her own duties and responsibilities. In such a case the court could consider the appointment of an intermediary.

If it is acceptable that the task of such an officer is to help ensure that a transnational insolvency proceeding is operated in accordance with the goals of the Global Principles and the provisions either set in a protocol or by the court's decision, it should be discussed what types of actions he could take, for instance to ensure that he will receive the necessary information, to facilitate adequate information exchanges between the administrators involved or to allow him to mediate between administrators to help in solving possible disagreements. Topics open for discussion include:

- whether the court retains jurisdiction or may need to postpone any actions or orders;
- whether an intermediary should have any binding powers;
- whether he will be able to alert the court to potential problems;
- whether he can request the court to instruct the administrator in a certain way;
- whether such decisions can be appealed; and
- what his/her position would be with regard to the other courts which may be involved in the case.

The alternative presented here should be measured against certain key factors which can indicate which alternative seems the best, given the circumstances of the case. Key indicators include:

- the avoidance of heavy costs for courts (larger cross-border insolvency cases concern businesses in financial distress and – in the end – these businesses should be responsible for resolving their own problems);
- the general need to decide in insolvency matters with urgency and speed;
- the general preference of disputants for confidentiality and to limit court involvement;
- the wish to save resources for the insolvent estate;
- ensuring easier implementation (e.g. of a cross-border rescue plan);
- streamlining notices to creditors, as well as general business considerations, such as gaining time and efficiency and tapping on available expertise.[16]

[16] These indicators in general also reflect a more recent trend in many Western legal systems to reduce the problem of excessive and expensive resort to court proceedings, see N. Andrews, The Modern Civil Process, Mohr Siebeck, 2008.

Towards a Convention?

Legal and practical obstacles also stand in the way to what is generally felt to be a workable solution to the effective and efficient operation of cross-border insolvency proceedings. Courts miss or overlook the power or are perceived to overlook the power to communicate or coordinate related insolvency cases. The solution seems simple: in these countries, governments should address this question with some urgency. As judicial cooperation in cross-border insolvency cases is seen as such a vital component, it seems that a set of globally accepted rules concerning a court's jurisdiction and preferably also certain rules regarding procedure, hearing of parties involved etc. is essential. My colleague Professor Fletcher has made a similar address, related to the preparation of a convention for the unification of the relevant parts of conflict of laws, as applicable to international insolvency.[17] In his suggestion, the Hague Conference on Private International Law would be best suited as an organisation to perform this task. Although I have supported his view, the lessons to be learned from the present step-by-step (incremental) approach, mainly concerning procedural, rather than substantial issues, may make it more realistic to provide courts with a solid back up.

The world of international insolvency is packed with soft law documents. They amount to a striking demonstration of the globalisation of commercial activity in the present era. They too have raised awareness internationally of the need to address the issues associated with insolvency in a cross-border context. Until now, states have only recently started to provide regulation for international businesses experiencing financial difficulties which have cross-border effects. Many jurisdictions have enacted a variety of provisions related to cross-border coordination by administrators and only in some instances by courts. Given the essential role courts play the present rules of play should be supported by more robust rules for the cross-border judicial coordination of cross-border cases. I respectfully propose that The Hague Conference on Private International Law should take a leading role here. I think such a convention, given the indispensable role of courts in insolvency cases, is desirable and feasible. My tentative view is that its contents should be limited in that it formulates fundamental rules and principles and allows the use of protocols, in which case specific details according to a certain format can be arranged. [18] Given its track record, the Hague Conference could deliver the most adequate form of regulation, i.e. a convention, so that at least courts should be provided with a sound and well-tailored framework for

---

[17] I. Fletcher, "The Quest for Global Insolvency Law: A Challenge for Our Time", Inaugural Lecture at University College London, 2002, in: M. Freemen (ed.), Current Legal Problems 2002, Volume 55, Oxford University Press. See also I. Fletcher, Insolvency in Private International Law, 2nd ed., 2005, 9.19.

[18] S. Taylor, "The Use of Protocols in Cross Border Insolvency Cases", in: K. Pannen (ed.), European Insolvency Regulation, Berlin: De Gruyter Recht, 2007, 686, suggests the creation of a standardised protocol as a template and a benchmark to facilitate higher levels of cooperation.

international cooperation.[19] International practice and present opinion demonstrates the ability and willingness that (insolvency) judges possess to play the vital role in applying an effective and efficient insolvency system. Such a convention should ensure that all stakeholders in a restructuring or insolvency have the information they need to make informed decisions, should adopt procedural safeguards to ensure the integrity of all judgments given and should in all act as an aid for judges to navigate in the uncharted waters of international insolvency.

---

[19] For a similar approach, see the Address made by Hon. Chief Justice of New South Wales, Australia, J.J. Spigelman, "Cross-Border Insolvency: Cooperation or conflict?" (INSOL International Annual Regional Conference, Shanghai, 16 September 2008 (on file with author).

The Intersection of Insolvency and Company Laws

PART III
INTERSECTION OF INSOLVENCY
AND COMPANY LAWS

Chapter 7

Pensions and Insolvency Law: A Functional Comparison of US, UK and Canadian Legal Regimes

Ron Davis

Introduction

Following decades of tax and pension law regulation of private sector employer-sponsored pension plans, two insolvency risks remain for plan members. The first ("contribution arrears") is a failure by the employer to make contributions required by either the terms of a defined contribution plan or by the actuarial calculations of the normal cost of the defined benefit plan. The second risk ("funding deficiency") is confined to defined benefit pension plans, which are defined by the promise that a plan member will receive a certain amount per month for the rest of his or her life when they retire. The risk is that the assumptions about future events used in the actuarial calculations of the cost in a defined benefit plan are sufficiently different from the actual events to cause a plan to be underfunded in relation to its liabilities at the time of an employer insolvency and potential termination of the plan. Pension legislation attempts to remedy this type of funding deficiency by requiring a plan sponsor to eliminate it within a specified period of years by making special additional payments, in addition to the contributions required to pay normal costs. However, if an employer does not make all of the special payments, a funding deficiency will still exist when the employer becomes insolvent and the plan is terminated.

The paper discusses whether or not these two risks are addressed by the insolvency regime and, if not, what other means exist to address the risks. The issue is addressed by looking at how these issues are addressed in the 2008 changes in Canada's insolvency law and comparing them to the US and UK risk mitigation measures. Prior to the 2008 reforms, claims resulting from both risks were general unsecured claims in liquidation proceedings. [1] In Canada, recovery

---

[1] Abraham v. Canadian Admiral Corp. (Receiver of), [1993] O.J. No. 1401, 20 C.B.R. (3d) 257 (Ont. Ct. (Gen. Div.)), this ground of the decision affd [1998] O.J. No. 1298, 2 C.B.R. (4th) 243 (Ont. C.A.); Re Ivaco Inc., [2005] O.J. No. 3337, 12 C.B.R. (5th) 213 at para. 13 (Ont. Sup. Ct. J.), affd [2006] O.J. No. 4152(Ont. C.A.).

rates for such claims are very low. [2] Since both types of claims originate from statutory obligations, any compromise in a restructuring proceeding required the sanction of the applicable regulator as well as the affected plan members.

The 2008 amendments completely reverse the situation concerning the contribution arrears risk. The new provisions give pension contribution arrears (but not funding deficiency payments) a statutory secured claim for the unpaid contributions over all of the employer's assets. This claim ranks fourth in preference after a claim for unpaid wages (up to $2,000 per employee) and unremitted tax deductions and ahead of ordinary secured claims.[3] However, funding deficiency claims still remain general unsecured claims in liquidation proceedings. In restructuring proceedings, the new amendments now require that an acceptable plan for payment of contribution arrears must be part of any proposal or arrangement, subject to the possibility of a negotiated variation approved by the pension regulator.[4] This treatment of contribution arrears can be compared with the treatment of contribution arrears in the US and UK insolvency regimes, where there are some similarities and differences, but in both of those countries, funding deficiencies are not as risky for plan members as they are in Canada, despite being treated as general unsecured claims.

A detailed review of the legislative schemes concerning contribution arrears and funding deficiency for pension plans in insolvency proceedings in these two countries is provided in the paper on which this presentation is based. However, it should be sufficient for this summary to provide the following comparative table:

Risk	US	UK	Canada Pre-Reform	Canada Post-Reform
Contribution Arrears	Effectively unsecured (although secured claim provided under pension legislation)	2nd Rank Claim	Unsecured Claim	4th Rank Secured Claim

[2] K. Davis and J. Ziegel, "Assessing the Economic Impacts of a New Priority Scheme for Unpaid Wage Earners and Suppliers of Goods and Services", prepared for the Corporate Law Policy Directorate (30 April 1998), online: Industry Canada strategis.ic.gc.ca/SSG/cl00150e.html#BIA_consult at Appendix B, Table 3. Employees received an average of only 7% of their general unsecured claims.

[3] *Bankruptcy and Insolvency Act,* R.S.C. 1985, c. B-3, (hereinafter cited as BIA), s. 81.5 & 81.6.

[4] BIA, s. 81.5 and Companies' Creditors Arrangement Act, R.S.C. 1985, c. C-36, s. 6(5) ("CCAA").

[5] F. Stewart, "Benefit Protection: Priority Creditor Rights for Pension Funds", OECD *Working Papers on Insurance and Private Pensions,* No. 6 (Paris: OEDC Publishing, 2007) at 24; D.R. Korobkin, "Employee Interests in Bankruptcy", (1996) 4 *American Bankruptcy Institute Law Review* 5 at 21-22 points out that a pre-petition stay prevents the PBGC from perfecting a post-petition lien.

Funding Deficiency	Unsecured PBGC Guarantee $47,000+ Maximum	Unsecured PPF Guarantee £27,000+ Maximum	Unsecured Claim (Except Ontario PBGF Guarantee $12,000 Max)	Unsecured Claim (Except Ontario PBGF Guarantee $12,000 Max)

As can be seen, both the US and UK have chosen to deal with the funding deficiency risk outside of the insolvency regime through a mandatory self-insurance provision of their pension legislation. In contrast, Canada, although it has granted a super-priority secured claim to contribution arrears, it only has a self-insurance provision in one of its provinces, Ontario. The question arises, why the differences between these countries' strategies for dealing with these two insolvency risks? Looking at the chart, one sees that the contribution arrears risk has been addressed through (more or less effective) attempts to provide increased priority to such claims. In contrast, funding deficiency claims are not addressed in insolvency legislation, but rather by insurance provisions in pension legislation, except in Canada, where only one province has an insurance fund, and its payments are quite minimal when compared with the US and UK insurance arrangements.

Choice of Insolvency Remedy for Contribution Arrears

A number of rationales have been discussed for granting preferences to employees for their unpaid wages and benefits.[6] However, there are two additional reasons why one might choose an insolvency remedy, rather than a non-insolvency remedy for contribution arrears: the non-payment was a result of a deliberate and illegal choice; and, there is the real potential that the insolvent employer's assets will be able to satisfy the claim.

Pension legislation in all three countries requires regular contributions be made to both defined contribution and defined benefit plans. Any contribution arrears will thus likely involve a deliberate decision by the employer to postpone or avoid remitting the contributions in order to use the funds to keep the business going. Such an action amounts to a preference in favour of the non-pension plan creditors that is contrary to the statutory obligations of the employer. Thus, granting contribution arrears claims a preference in the claims over remaining assets can be seen as an attempt to recognize that the non-payment may have been the result of preferences granted to other creditors while committing an offence. To the extent that insolvency law can serve to provide appropriate incentives to financially distressed employers and their creditors to comply with statutory obligations, granting a post-insolvency preference for those statutory obligations can proved such incentives. In addition, in the US and UK, the ability to collect any of these wrongfully withheld contributions can relieve some of the financial burden on their national benefit guarantee funds.

[6] These are summarized in D. Baird and R. Davis, Chapter Four "Labour Issues", in A. Duggan and S. Ben-Ishai, eds. Canadian Bankruptcy and Insolvency Law (Toronto: Lexis-Nexis Butterworths, 2007) at pp. 69–70.

A second reason why the insolvency remedy makes sense in the case of contribution arrears is that, unlike most solvency deficiencies, there is a real potential of recovery from the insolvent employer's assets. The point here is simply that the typical contribution arrears claim is of a significantly lower order of magnitude than those in a funding deficiency with the former being possibly in the thousands to millions range and the latter being in the tens of millions to billions range. It would make little sense to have an insolvency remedy that will not have a significant impact in many insolvency proceedings, subject to the ability of the relevant courts to curb efforts by other creditors to evade this remedy's impact through pre-petition manoeuvring. However, neither of these two rationales makes sense in the case of the funding deficiency risk.

Choice of Non-insolvency Remedy for Solvency Deficiency

All three countries have chosen to deal with solvency deficiency risk outside of the insolvency regime. Two reasons why legislators would choose this route rather than an insolvency remedy are: solvency deficiencies may arise without any wrongdoing or breach of statutory obligations on the employer's part; and, the dimensions of the claim are likely to far exceed the available assets, especially in the case of mature pension plans.

Funding deficiencies will not arise in a defined contribution plan in the absence of contributions arrears because the risks that give rise to such deficiencies are all borne by the plan members in such plans. In a defined benefit plan, a funding deficiency can arise when one or more of the variables on which an actuary has based his calculation of the amount of contributions vary adversely when compared to the assumptions used by the actuary. Recent examples of such adverse variations involved lower than assumed long-term interest rates and investment returns. Clearly, providing there was no improper behaviour involved in the choice of assumptions for the calculations or the valuation of the plan, there is no element of deliberate choice to underfund by the employer.[7] Indeed, it is difficult to characterize the situation as one involving a preference for one creditor over another. Thus, the connection to an insolvency law remedy involving post-petition preference is weak.

In addition, unlike the amount of pension contributions, which are relatively fixed and easily discoverable by other creditors deciding whether or not to grant credit, the amount of a solvency deficiency is quite volatile and would make any credit granting decision an very uncertain exercise.[8] This concern about

[7] Where there are allegations that the employer deliberately instructed an actuary to use assumptions about plan asset values that would allow it to avoid having to make solvency deficiency payments, this may involve breach of fiduciary duty as a plan administrator: Morneau Sobeco Limited Partnership v. Aon Consulting Inc. (2008), 65 C.C.P.B. 293, 291 D.L.R. (4th) 314 (Ont. C.A.) leave to appeal application dismissed 4 September 2008 (SCC).

[8] K. Ambachtsheer, "Cleaning Up the Pensions Mess: Why It Will Take More than Money", C.D. Howe Institute Backgrounder No. 78, February 2004, reports that, based on a review of the financial results of 68 large Canadian pension plans, their funded status had deteriorated by almost 30% over the three years from 2000–2002.

disruption of capital markets has been cited as one of the reasons the UK did not change the order of priority for pension claims in its as discussed in the 2004 Green Paper on Pensions.[9]

Finally, the sheer size of some pension fund solvency deficiencies would dwarf the value of available assets of a financially distressed employer and therefore would not lead to any meaningful recovery, irrespective of priority of such a claim in an insolvency distribution rule. For example, in the Stelco insolvency proceeding, pension liabilities for existing and retired employees exceeded several billion dollars.[10] In Air Canada, the CCAA monitor reported that the estimated shortfall in funding of the Air Canada pension plans was $1.8 billion dollars if the pension plan was terminated immediately.[11] Thus, a more effective response to the solvency deficiency risk is some form of risk pooling or insurance which addresses the no-fault nature of the risk, the likelihood that post-insolvency employer assets will be inadequate to address the more severe forms of deficiency and the inability of employees of individual employers to diversify their risk without moving from employer to employer.[12]

Canada's Choices

What might explain the differences between Canada and the other two jurisdictions? Clearly the federal government has no principled grounds for opposing government intervention to protect the pension benefits of employees of an insolvent employer, as demonstrated by their willingness to implement the super priority for pension contribution arrears. However, there are some factors unique to Canada which, when combined with the nature of the insurance remedy, may explain why there is no nationwide pension benefit insurance scheme.

Canada's Constitutional Division of Legislative Authority

Unlike the UK which has a unitary legislature and the US, where the federal government has legislative authority over both insolvency and pensions in the private sector, Canada has split constitutional legislative authority over these subjects. The federal Parliament has legislative authority over matters of bankruptcy and insolvency, while the provincial legislatures exercise legislative authority over employee benefits in the private sector. Thus, while the ultimate impact of funding deficiencies manifest themselves in insolvency proceedings; the federal government has no direct legislative access to the pension benefit

---

[9] F. Stewart, Benefit Protection supra, note 5 at 22.

[10] Re Stelco Inc. [2005] O. J. No. 1171, 75 O.R. (3d) 5 (Ont. C.A.).

[11] Eighth Report of Monitor, July 31, 2003, Air Canada, Re, No. 03-CL-4932 ((Ont. S.C.J. (Commercial List)) 2003), paragraphs 15 & 16, this was an increase of approximately $500 million over a previous estimate, an increase that was attributed to the decline in long-term interest rates by Air Canada's actuaries.

[12] N.L. Nielson, "Insurance Against Plan and Sponsor Failure", Expert Commission on Pensions Research Report no. 6 at 7-8, copy available at: http://www.pensionreview.on.ca/english/summaries/6Nielson.html.

insurance remedy. Any nationwide implementation of such a remedy would require extensive negotiations with provincial governments, especially in light of the potentially large fiscal impact of such a scheme on provincial budgets. Thus, the federal government has moved in the legislative field in which it can act directly to respond to the political pressure from the electorate to do something about the threat to pension benefits, but its only easily available remedy will only remedy a small part of the threat – contribution arrears.

The Nature of Insurance

The second possible reason why the federal government has not pursued the issue with the provincial governments is that even if it were to provide fiscal backing to provincial pension benefit insurance schemes, it would lack the legislative authority needed to protect itself from the hazards that accompany insurance provision. As a number of authors have pointed out, the main argument against pension guarantee funds is moral hazard. The moral hazard is that employers may engage in increasingly risky behaviour because they know that irrespective of the results of the risk, pension benefits will be paid by the guarantee fund. Some examples of risky behaviour would include increasing the benefits promised by the plan without regard for its assets or contribution levels, reducing contribution rates or pursuing a risky investment strategy.[14]

Pension legislation can address the moral hazard problem by requiring contribution rates be calculated by professional actuaries according to a professional standard, making recent benefit increases ineligible for the guarantee, or charging higher premiums for plans with more severe underfunding problems. In the Canadian constitutional context, however, legislative authority over such controls on moral hazard lies in the hands of the provincial governments, not the federal government. It would make no sense for the federal government to offer a form of fiscal guarantee of a national pension benefit guarantee plan while lacking the legislative tools to control the hazards of an insurance scheme it has agreed to fund.

This important difference in the constitutional legislative authority in Canada, in comparison with the UK and US may offer at least a partial explanation of why the federal government has not implemented a pension benefit guarantee plan together with its other insolvency reforms that benefit employees. Any such plan would require extensive negotiations with the 10 provinces as well as some agreement on conditions to control moral hazard and there is real danger that an insistence on such conditions would be seen by some provinces as unwarranted interference with their legislative authority. In contrast, in both the UK and US, legislative authority over all aspects of the solvency deficiency problem is located in a single legislative body. Seen in this light, the prospects for a nation-wide

[13] N.L. Nielson, "Insurance Against Plan and Sponsor Failure" supra at 20; F. Stewart, "Benefit Security Pension Fund Guarantee Schemes", *OECD Working Papers on Insurance and Private Pensions* No. 5 (Paris: OECD Publishing, 2007) at 6.

[14] F. Stewart, *loc. cit.*

pension benefit guarantee scheme seem remote for Canadian plan members, except in Ontario, and even in that province, the scheme's low maximum guarantee does not provide much comfort for plan members contemplating a solvency deficiency in their pension fund.

Impact of the reforms

Clearly, the increased priority and granting of a statutory secured claim for pension contribution arrears claims in Canada's insolvency reforms will greatly enhance the likelihood of recovery. This likelihood is reduced, however, by the simultaneous granting of a higher ranking statutory secured claim for unpaid wages to a maximum of $2,000 per employee. Although the unpaid wages claim statutory security is effective over a more limited amount of the insolvent employer's assets – its "current assets" – it has the potential to absorb a significant amount of the employer's available assets, as does the next ranking secured claim for unremitted source deductions for income tax and employment insurance.[15] Thus, although the potential for increased recovery exists, it will be entirely dependent on the size of the insolvent employer's estate and whether or not management continued timely remissions of source deductions and payment of wages.

There remains the potential for another development that may also prove beneficial for pension plan members; increased monitoring by non-statutory secured creditors. Some scholars have been critical of the relatively poor job of monitoring performed by secured creditors because they are only concerned with monitoring the assets that comprise their security.[16] However, with the creation of the new statutory super priority securities for unpaid wages, source deductions and pension contribution arrears, secured creditors can no longer rest comfortably providing the specific assets over which they hold security are intact. These assets will subject to prior claims by the statutory secured claims and if they are insufficient to satisfy both the statutory claims and the secured creditor claims, then the secured creditors will become general unsecured creditors. In view of this potential, general secured creditors will have incentives to monitor the debtor firm for financial distress in the same manner as other unsecured creditors. They can insist on similar covenants to those used to monitor debtors by banks giving unsecured lines of credit that some scholars believe make those banks efficient monitors of the creditor.[17] They may also insist on some mechanisms to assure timely remittances and payments of the amounts subject to the new statutory priorities, in order to protect the assets over which they hold security from the statutory secured claims. It will be important to gather empirical evidence of effects on the credit market, monitoring efforts by secured creditors and amounts collected for pension contribution arrears in the period following the new reforms

---

[15] BIA, s. 81.3 & 81.4.

[16] B. Adler, "An Equity-Agency Solution to the Bankruptcy-Priority Puzzle" (1993) J. of Legal Stud. 73.

[17] G. Triantis and R.J. Daniels, "The Role of Debt in Interactive Corporate Governance" (1995) 83 California Law Review 1073.

in order to determine the effects of this legislative initiative. This research may also serve as a catalyst for the creation of a more effective protective regime based on insurance principles through negotiations between the provincial and federal governments.

Chapter 8

Credit Derivatives: Risk Management, Control Rights and the Implications for Insolvency Workout Proceedings

Janis Sarra

Introduction

Structured financial products play an important role in today's global economy. However, events in September 2008 have highlighted new challenges in respect of their use, particularly as firms become insolvent.

The traditional notion of debt involves fixed return on investments, control rights, contractual covenants, and default rights, all of which create incentives for debtor companies to meet their credit obligations and allow creditors to protect their economic interests, particularly as a debtor company slides into financial distress. On insolvency, creditors can exercise default control rights based on their economic interest in the debtor. The debtor company requires the support of creditors if it is to successfully restructure. In recent years, however, creditors, in particular, lending institutions, have hedged their economic risk through credit derivatives, a generic term for over-the-counter financial instruments that allow parties to transfer or assume credit risk. There are numerous kinds of credit derivatives, such as credit default swaps ("CDS"), collateralized debt obligations ("CDO"), full and index trades, and credit-linked notes. Credit derivatives are classified as either single or multi-name basket products. Single name credit derivatives are targeted on the credit worthiness of a single reference entity. Multi-name products hedge the risk of clustered defaults in a portfolio.[1]

The Nature of Credit Derivatives

The global market for credit derivatives estimated to be between US$30 trillion and US$70 trillion, depending on how it is measured. The most common form of credit derivatives are credit default swaps, many written on well-known corporate and sovereign names. CDS grew rapidly, originally because they were an effective

---

[1] E. Murphy, J. Sarra and M. Creber, "Credit Derivatives in Canadian Insolvency Proceedings, 'The Devil will be in the Details", in J. Sarra, ed., Annual Review of Insolvency Law, 2006 (Toronto: Carswell) at 187-234.

a risk management tool for financial institutions. In basic single-name CDS, the protection buyer buys from a protection seller, protection against the credit risk associated with a principal amount (notional amount) of a debt or guarantee obligation (reference obligation) of a debtor (reference entity) for a specified period (tenor). The CDS is a bilateral agreement that allows a party to transfer its credit risk in respect of the reference asset or reference entity, that it may or may not own, to another party without actually selling the asset; for example, a bondholder hedges "spread risk", the risk that the company's credit profile will worsen, and/or "default risk". Principal participants in the market include commercial banks, investment banks, hedge funds, pension funds and insurance companies, as both risk sellers and risk takers. Protection buyers use CDS to manage particular market exposures in order to diversify their own investment portfolios.

While credit derivatives provide for the transfer of credit risk, they are complex products with a short history of experience. There is also an active trading market for CDS. The use of credit derivatives grew in popularity in a relatively benign economic environment; and now with current financial crisis, there are new challenges.

The key elements of a CDS contract are identification of the reference entity or asset, description of the reference obligation, selection of credit events, and specification of mechanisms of settlement. Conceptually, terms are subject to negotiation; however, in practice, most credit derivatives are over-the-counter commodity products with industry wide standards set by the International Swaps and Derivatives Association (ISDA). Most credit derivative transactions, including most CDS, are not funded, but may be subject to margin and collateral arrangements depending on the counterparty.

Another part of the structured financial products market is collateralized debt obligations. The shortage of available protection sellers for banks seeking to free up their regulatory capital contributed to development of CDO. Typically, a bank transfers a bundle of credits to special investment vehicles. The special investment vehicle sells senior CDO and then multiple tranches to investors, each tranche with higher risk and higher potential yield. Where the structure of CDO did not remove credit risk while being flexible to accommodate fluctuating loans at the customer level, "synthetic" CDO capital structures were developed. The synthetic structure responded to investors searching for enhanced yields where they were willing to assume higher risk. The result of these developments was a degree of management of risk, but separation of creditors' economic interest in the debtor from formal rights, what Professors Hu and Black have called "decoupling".[2]

---

[2] H. Hu and B. Black, "Debt, Equity and Hybrid Decoupling; Governance and Systemic Risk Implications", forthcoming 2008 European Financial Management 17.

The Role of Credit Derivatives in the Financial Crisis

If the development of these products was meeting a market need, what is their role in the current financial crisis and why should insolvency scholars, practitioners and judges be concerned? Essentially, the existence of credit derivatives, and in particular, CDS, in insolvency proceedings has changed the dynamic and the economic interests that are at the bargaining table.

By way of backdrop, global credit derivatives exposures by ratings shifted downward in recent years. In 2002, 36% of all credit derivatives globally were rated at AA or AAA, whereas only 8% were rated as below investment grade. Just four years later, in 2006, only 17% of credit derivatives globally were rated at AA or AAA, whereas 31% were now rated as below investment grade.[3] Counterparty risk was heavily concentrated among the top 20 global banks and broker dealers, including Bear Sterns, Lehman Brothers, AIG, Merrill Lynch and Royal Bank of Scotland.[4] Among the U.S. banks, 77% of the credit derivative volume in 2006 was carried out by Citibank, Bank of America, Wachovia and HSBC USA. This increased exposure was the first factor that shifted the nature of these products.

Second, the banks' market share declined in roughly the same period as hedge funds increasingly took a greater share of both the buy side and sell side of the market. In 2000, banks accounted 81% of the buy side and 63% of the sell side of market share, that number dropping to 59% and 44% respectively by 2006. Hedge funds went from 3% of the market on the buy side in 2000 to 28% market share in 2006. As a seller, their market share grew from 5% to 32% market share in the same period.[5] Those derivatives were then hedged in further credit derivatives in multiples of the value of the originating reference entities. The hedge funds were a major driver of change in the market. The reasons for a move down the credit curve included tight spreads; as margins squeezed at the upper end of the credit curve, to maintain returns, investors shifted to more speculative investment grades and unrated exposures.[6] In 2006, co-authors Creber, Murphy and I concluded that the adequacy of any collateral requirements had not been tested during period of real credit stress or market dislocation.[7] What a difference a day makes....or a couple of years....? Today we are watching a number of icons collapse into insolvency, Lehman Brothers, Bear Stearns, Merrill Lynch, Fannie Mae, Wachovia and AIG.

The third shift was a growth in the speculative trading of CDS. Rather than being used as a risk management tool, with positive contributions to the availability of capital and the hedging of risk, much of the market has become a speculative trading market. This market operates both within and outside of insolvency.

---

[3] Fitch Ratings, discussed in E. Murphy, J. Sarra and M. Creber, *supra,* note 1.
[4] *Ibid.*
[5] British Bankers Association, Credit Derivatives Report, 2006.
[6] For a more comprehensive discussion of these issues, see J. Sarra, *Credit Derivatives Market Design, Creating Fairness and Sustainability,* (2008) London: NSFM) at 3.
[7] E. Murphy, J. Sarra and M. Creber, *supra,* note 1.

Restructuring proceedings of debtors referenced in CDS are of interest to the originator and the current beneficiary of such a derivative as the outcome crystallizes the obligations under a derivative. If there is a direct relationship between the debt and payment obligation under a swap, the derivative contract itself represents the economic interest. However, many outstanding derivative contracts may aggregate five to ten times the value of creditor claims.

Control Rights Issues

There are numerous issues raised by the recent developments. Here, I focus on control rights, specifically, how CDS may affect the behaviour and motivations of various stakeholders of a distressed business enterprise during restructuring. Most critically, the existence of CDS in respect of an insolvent debtor corporation can cause greater complexity and uncertainty in restructuring proceedings, as the real economic interests of stakeholders is not transparent. Moreover, some parties to workout negotiations change in quick succession where CDS are physically settled. If a restructuring is attempted in an environment of general economic decline, where numerous credit events are occurring affecting a significant number of CDS, those challenges may cause the restructuring to fail. The legal and operational risks may impair the restructuring process. Settlement of derivative contracts may be complicated by capital structure changes in respect of the reference entity through mergers or restructuring, with the possibility that the debt of a reference entity becomes debt of different entities. There can be a lack of certainty in the credit derivative market as to which default risk is being transferred.[8] Although most CDS are primarily standard form contracts with several important terms negotiated, early cases suggest that when the reference entity becomes insolvent, there are disputes in respect of the protection period, the precise reference obligation, the deliverable obligation, and whether a credit event has actually occurred.[9] There is legal uncertainty regarding the interpretation and enforcement of credit derivative contracts. Moreover, there is asymmetry of knowledge of the risk as between an originating lender transferring credit risk to purchasers.

In insolvency restructuring proceedings, the classic paradigm is that stakeholders with an economic interest in the debtor company are the parties with the greatest interest and arguably, influence, in the restructuring. However, given the existence of credit derivatives, particularly CDS, the corporate debtor may have hidden creditors and/or creditors holding less economic interest than the face value of their claims or even a negative economic interest. Hence the existence of credit derivatives may complicate the classic paradigm by potentially affecting the composition and motivations of various stakeholders. On insolvency, one moral hazard is that a creditor that has material holdings of credit derivatives may have

---

[8] Although it is assisted at least in part by the Reference Entity Database.

[9] For a discussion of early cases, see E. Murphy, J. Sarra and M. Creber, supra, note 1.

economic interests that potentially encourage it to cause a default to occur so that there is a credit event.[10]

There are many factors that can affect the motivation and behaviour of stakeholders in an insolvency restructuring, given their economic interests; yet the creditor that has hedged its risk through a credit derivative is arguably in a different position in the restructuring proceeding, as there is a lack of transparency in respect of whether in fact there are economic interests at risk. This observation is not to suggest that credit derivatives drive behaviour in all cases; rather, it is a growing phenomenon with the move to cash settlements and growth of the market.

Under physical settlement of a CDS, the single institution from which a debtor company borrowed and believed it had a credit relationship results now in multiplicity of intermediaries and counterparties as CDS settle.[11] The insolvent company may not even appreciate before commencing a restructuring proceeding that it is a reference entity. Cascading swaps means multiple rapid changes to who holds the claim, making it difficult for a debtor company to establish who has a claim and thus the party with which it should be negotiating.[12] The debtor can suddenly be dealing with literally hundreds of new claimants. Given settlement time lags, where the protection seller with each physical settlement becomes the party at the restructuring bargaining table, the company's ability to devise a viable business plan can be hindered, particularly problematic if there is urgency in devising a plan because of a liquidity crisis or the need to maintain customer goodwill.[13] If the original creditor was only partially hedged under the credit derivative, then with physical settlement, there are now two or more parties with financial exposure for a debt that previously involved one creditor. Due to the trading volumes, there is the potential for this effect to be exponential. The potential for credit derivatives to cause a "revolving door" effect, combined with the changing stakeholders due to claims purchasing by distressed debt purchasers, hedge funds and private equity funds, means that the debtor may face insurmountable challenges in trying to build consensus on a restructuring plan and in trying to garner the requisite support of creditors. In Canada, the required support is a majority in number and two-thirds the value of claims, as required by both the *Companies' Creditors Arrangement Act (CCAA)* for a plan of compromise and arrangement and the *Bankruptcy and Insolvency Act (BIA)* for a proposal.

Cash settlement of CDS poses different kinds of challenges for restructuring. Unlike insurance, no title to the claim passes and there is no right of subrogation. With cash settlement, the protection buyer that is a creditor of the insolvent company continues to be the party with the legal claim, although at a reduced or eliminated financial exposure.[14] The debtor and other creditors have no

---

[10] This observation is not to lose sight of the fact that in a cash settlement, the protection buyer still has whatever it paid for the protection "at risk" in the insolvency proceeding.

[11] J. Sarra, supra, note 6.

[12] Ibid.

[13] Ibid.

[14] Where there are cash settled credit default swaps, on occurrence of a credit event, the CDS may be settled by

notice or knowledge of the reduced exposure. If the creditor is fully hedged, there will be little incentive to engage in constructive negotiations for a restructuring plan. This level of disengagement may be problematic for the restructuring. While in some cases, there can be an active market for derivatives during a restructuring where credit derivatives holders are also direct creditors and take an active and constructive role in workout negotiations, the converse can also occur. The financial institution with which the debtor company has had an operating lending relationship may be less interested in advancing further credit in form of post commencement or exit financing if it has no ongoing financial interest in the debtor. The creditor may actually have over-coverage and thus a negative economic interest, materially benefitting if the restructuring fails. Yet parties to the restructuring currently have no information on the economic interest held by those parties hedged through a credit derivative.[16]

Accordingly, a debtor company may find the creditor that is hedged under a CDS adamant in its refusal to agree to amendments to its credit arrangement such as a payment change or deferral and changes to covenants that would otherwise trigger a default or obligation acceleration. In addition, protection buying creditors will be unlikely to consent to the extension of the maturity date beyond the protection period unless a credit event has already occurred or the extension itself qualifies as a credit event.[17] These motivations may complicate the efforts of distressed companies to negotiate arrangements with their creditors at the early stages of distress in an attempt to restructure outside of formal insolvency proceedings. Moreover, a claims trader creditor may be seen as having a new, speculative and short term interest in the debtor. Having acquired its position when the debtor company is already in financial difficulty, it is often hedging against the speculative outcome of restructuring process.[18] Such a creditor, perhaps holding a deciding vote, has little interest in the long term viability of the company.

A number of jurisdictions have granted exemptions for derivatives from mandatory stays under insolvency laws because of an emphasis on maintaining marketability and the important public policy goal of global financial stability. However, the continued trading of derivatives in cases where settlement is based on the debtor's insolvency or filing of restructuring proceedings can cause further financial instability of the market in the name of preserving liquidity and makes restructuring difficult for debtor companies. In this respect, there is a tension between two broader public policy goals. On the one hand, Basel II capital rules require the ability to terminate, net and realize on collateral in order to allow institutions to take offsetting transactions into account for capital purposes.[19] If parties cannot close out, they face exposure on their off-setting trades, which can

determining the value of the underlying debt instrument through an ISDA-run or similar auction, whereby the protection seller pays the protection buyer for its estimated loss based on the value established in the auction or where a value can be determined based on post credit event bids for the debt product.

[15] J. Sarra, *supra,* note 6 at 13.

[16] Ibid.

[17] In order that they can realize on the value of the CDS.

[18] J. Sarra, *supra,* note 6 at 15.

[19] Basel Committee on Banking Supervision, International Convergence of Capital Measurement and Capital Standards: a Revised Framework, June 2004, www.bis.org/publ/bcbs107.htm (Basel II).

cause greater financial problems in the market. On the other hand, the move towards rehabilitation in insolvency laws globally is driven by the recognition that liquidation can often leave value on the table that would have meant greater realizations for subordinated secured creditors, unsecured creditors and employees, as well as positive ripple effects in the local economy that can be realized by preservation of economic activity in the community.[20] Both are important public policy goals and both require consideration in devising a going forward structure of the market.

The normative justification for carving out derivatives from stays under restructuring proceedings is unclear, given the shift from their risk management function to speculative product.[21] As the bailouts of recent weeks have illustrated, there is a broader public interest in how the global derivatives market is to operate effectively. Interests affected are beyond capital markets participants, and regulation is needed to ensure that there is transparency in the nature of economic exposure and underlying risk. There should be a public policy debate on whether there is a need to design new principles to account for the separation of economic and legal interest in context of insolvency proceedings.

Another aspect of the insolvency proceedings that may be implicated, whether restructuring or liquidation, is possible remedies against third parties, for example, recipients of preferences or alleged violation of directors' fiduciary obligations or duty of care. These rights may be separated and become beneficially owned by or exercisable by or for different parties. The fully hedged creditor will be less concerned with the success or failure of the debtor company or with the optimal realization on secured collateral. Given that financial institutions may be fully or partially hedged through CDS, a key consideration at point of filing a proceeding, such as restructuring proceedings in Canada under the *CCAA* or the *BIA*, is whether the debtor corporation or any affiliated companies are reference entities in the credit derivative market. If so, then parties that are creditors for purposes of the insolvency proceeding may have a reduced or no debt exposure in the proceeding. Such creditors may also have undertaken other measures to hedge their risk, such as credit insurance or sub-participation agreements, as credit derivatives are but one of a number of relatively new financial products that shift the amount of exposure of creditors at the point of the debtor corporation's insolvency.

These observations are not to suggest that the market has failed to address some of its flaws itself. CDS protocols and index auctions have helpfully assisted in facilitating cash settlements. The purpose of such protocols is to offer market participants an efficient way to settle credit derivative transactions referencing.[22] For example, when Collins & Aikman filed for bankruptcy in 2005, there were concerns that there were not enough deliverable bonds to settle all the existing index-related contracts. To address this issue, the ISDA published the first

[20] J. Sarra, *supra*, note 6.
[21] J. Sarra, *supra*, note x.
[22] ISDA Protocols, International Swaps and Derivatives Association (ISDA), 2006, https://www.isdadocs.org/index.html.

protocols to amend the existing contracts for index-related trades to cash settlement from physical settlement on a multi-lateral basis, rather than through counterparty to counterparty negotiations, and to participate in an auction to determine the cash-settlement price of the defaulted bonds.[23] With the CDS outstanding greater by multiples than the volume of bonds issued, the bonds would have to be bought and sold numerous times in the market to settle the CDS, which would have created pressure to source bonds, raising the price of the bonds higher than the likely recovery value. Hence, the market developed credit event auctions, first to facilitate cash settlement and more recently, to allow for physical settlement on net open positions.[24]

The largest participants in the CDS market are financial institutions managing or removing risk from their lending portfolios. In a deteriorating credit market, CDS counterparties may challenge claims made under CDS by financial institutions who, with hindsight, are alleged to have had prior knowledge of deterioration of the credit or to have been in early stages of restructuring negotiation in which the financial institution would itself have had a material ability to influence the occurrence of a credit event. Parties holding large CDS positions may proceed to acquire creditor claims in order to position themselves so that they can cause a credit event to occur. These parties are difficult to identify, in terms of who there are and their rights to participate in the insolvency proceeding. There are also arguably now parties with an economic interest who may have no legal relationship with the restructuring debtor and may not be entitled to standing in the proceedings; for example, a protection seller under credit derivatives. The asymmetry of knowledge between the protection buyer when it is also a lender and the protection seller produces legal risks that have not been definitively resolved and could impede the restructuring process. There is also an issue of incomplete contracting in that there are outstanding interpretation issues in the ISDA confirmation and in the ISDA definitions.

Conclusion

In conclusion, the existence of credit default swap cover on a debtor may affect the interests and behaviour of stakeholders during workout negotiations and the structure and terms of a proposed restructuring plan. The interests of parties with a credit default swap position will differ depending on the amount and duration of the cover, the definition of credit events and the type of settlement agreed to. There is a need for some transparency so that other stakeholders appreciate those with real economic risks if the firm is liquidated. There is a need to re-link economic interest with the control rights in insolvency proceedings, in order to properly preserve some of the fundamental objectives of insolvency law; specifically, the efficient and effective realization of creditors' claims and the working out, where possible, of a viable going forward business plan for the financially distressed business enterprise.

[23] Nomura, CDS Recovery Basis, ISDA, 2006.
[24] ISDA Auction Process, 2008, www.isda.org.

Chapter 9

Transformation and Relation of Corporate Law and Liquidation in Terms of the European Approximation of Laws

Ilona Aszódi

Introduction

The revision of the regulations on corporate and company law was commenced in the summer of 2003. During the course of the more than two-year long work, the act on business association was re-codified, in which, among others, the following objectives and principles were established.

The European Charter for small enterprises was adopted in June 2000, which called on the member states to establish the economic, financial and legal environment enhancing the operation of companies, with special emphasis on the reduction of the administrative burdens of the foundation of companies and the length of the registration procedure, as well as the introduction of electronic corporate procedures.

The report of the committee led by Wim Kok, ex-Dutch Prime Minister was published in November 2004, which among others is about making the European Union the most dynamic and competitive knowledge-based economy of the world by 2010. For this to be achieved, it attached particular importance to the fact that the member states should drastically reduce the time, the administrative burdens and the costs of the foundation of companies by 2005.

The conditions of the comprehensive operation of companies should be established: while ensuring the publicity of companies in the widest range possible for the sake of the security of economic turnover and the interests of creditors.

- the law provides for the decision autonomy of the owners;
- reasonable and proportionate provisions should be enforced for the protection of creditors and investors. The new rules having been introduced, for example solvency test, represent a significant legislative act towards the protection of creditors representing a more efficient and real guarantee.

Domestic Procedures

During the course of legal supervision, the Court of Registration becomes entitled to order even a supervisor in order to restore the lawful operation of the company.

The termination of companies retaining their solvency without legal successor also belongs to the sphere of authority of the Courts of Registration. Sometimes, it means the legalised method of rescuing assets. The asset management procedure was also regulated taking the practical rules into consideration. It can only be performed in so far as, subsequent to a validly completed insolvency procedure, the asset of the terminated company not having been taken into account during the course of the liquidation procedure is revealed. The legislator regulated it no more in the insolvency law, but in the company and corporate law.

A company, if not insolvent and unless otherwise provided by the relevant regulations, may be wound up without legal successor by way of final settlement "proceedings". The proceedings may be opened by decision of the supreme body of the company or by decision of the competent Court of Registration in judicial supervision (involuntary final settlement). Proceedings may not be opened after a declaring the insolvencies of the company. The proceedings in progress shall be terminated when the company is ordered to go into liquidation. The proceedings may not be opened, or if already is in progress, it may not be concluded after a notice delivered by a criminal court or the competent Court of Registration concerning the company's indictment in criminal proceedings carrying possible criminal sanctions. The proceedings in progress may be concluded before the verdict delivered by the criminal court becomes operative, and company in question may not be stricken from the register before the criminal sanctions imposed in this verdict are carried out. The subject of proceedings is the assets held by the company affected at the time of the opening the proceedings, as well as all assets acquired during the proceeding. The time of the opening of the proceedings is the date fixed in the resolution on the termination of corporate existence without legal successor; this date must not precede the date of the resolution.

The supreme body of the company shall fix its decision, adopted according to the relevant regulations, to terminate the company's corporate existence without legal successor and to go into proceedings a resolution. The supreme body of the company shall lay down in its resolution the time of the opening of proceedings and shall appoint a receiver, and shall provide for the future of the legal entities in which the company maintains a final interest, as well as the foundations and non-governmental organizations which it participates. At the time the opening of proceedings, the company's executive officer shall be dismissed. After the opening of proceedings, the receiver shall be considered as the company's executive officer vested with independent power of representation.

Within a period of forty-five days following the time of the opening the proceedings the company's former executive officer shall prepare a report according to the Accounting Act for closing out the company's account effective as on the day preceding the time of the opening of proceedings, and shall perform the duties conferred upon him by accounting, taxation and other regulations, and shall hand these documents and all other documents and record of the company over to the receiver on or before the forty-fifth day following the time of the opening of proceedings.

The company's former executive officer shall be subject to civil liability according to the general provisions for damages resulting from his failure to discharge the duties or from his failure to meet the deadlines prescribed. In this event if the Court of Registration may impose a penalty, on one or more occasions, upon the former executive officer at the receiver's request of between HUF 50,000 and 500,000 within the framework of judicial oversight proceedings.

At the receiver's request, the Court of Registration may order the former executive officer, to cover the costs of the expert commissioned by the receiver to carry out the duties. The company's supreme may elect any person to serve as the receiver, if in conformity with the requirements set out for the executive officer, and if this person accepts the assignment. A suitable legal person or a business association lacking the legal status of a legal person may also be elected to serve as the receiver. The resolution on the termination of corporate existence without legal successor shall also provide for the receiver's remuneration, or shall assign the receiver to discharge these duties on a voluntary basis. The receiver shall exercise special care as generally expected from persons in such positions, serving the best interests of the company undergoing dissolution and the interests of creditors. The receiver shall be held liable in accordance with the general provisions of civil law for damages caused by any beach of his obligations.

The Court of Registration shall deliver a ruling ordering the opening of proceedings, and shall publish it in the Company Gazette. The main point of it is a notice to the creditors to notify their known claims to the receiver within forty days following the date of publication of the notice.

The receiver shall assess the company's financial position in the course of the proceedings, recover its claims, pay its debts, enforce its claims and discharge its obligations, and shall sell of its assets if necessary. the receiver shall distribute the assets remaining after the satisfaction of creditors among the members (shareholders) in cash or in kind, and shall terminate the company's operations. The company's supreme body may instruct the receiver to sell all or parts of the company's financial assets by public bidding or by way of auction. Final settlement shall be completed within three years following the time of the opening of the proceedings.

If a request for the cancellation of the company from the records is not submitted within three years, the company shall be subject to involuntary dissolution. The company's creditors shall notify their claims to the receiver within forty days following the date of publication of the notice. Claims must be notified also if the company affected is undergoing official or legal proceedings in connection with the claims in question. Delay to file the notice of claim shall not constitute their "death", however, following the approval of the closing balance sheet and the proposal for the distribution of assets, creditor's claims may only be satisfied according to the provisions governing facilities for the debts of the defunct company. If the receiver concludes on the basis of the adjusted opening balance sheet for the proceeding that the company's assets are insufficient to cover the creditors claims, and the members (shareholders) fail to supply the funds lacking within thirty days, a request for liquidation must be submitted without delay.

In the event of any illegal action or negligence by the receiver the other party may file a dissolution complaint during the period of proceedings of the receiver within eight days of gaining knowledge thereof, or within sixty days from the date of occurrence of the illegal action or negligence at the latest.

The supreme body shall adopt a resolution concerning the documents presented and on the subject of the distribution of assets, which may be for the assignment of rights and the transfer of liabilities, or for the assumption of the company's debts by others. The resolution, if necessary, shall contain provisions for the receiver's fee and on the bearing of the costs of dissolution, including the costs of storage of the company's documents and the costs arising in connection with the company's termination.

If the court, acting in its judicial supervisory competence, declares a company wound up, involuntary dissolution shall be ordered. Involuntary dissolution proceedings shall be conducted also if, according to substantive regulations, there are grounds for the termination of the company without legal successor or if the company did not conclude its final settlement within three years, or if it did not switch to the general provisions on dissolution.

In the course of involuntary dissolution the supreme body of the company shall have no competence to decide on the company's operation during the dissolution proceedings, or to terminate the dissolution proceedings. Following the time of the opening of dissolution proceedings the bodies of the company may not adopt any decision which is in contradiction with the objective of the dissolution.

The Competition Factor and Conclusion

The regulation of corporate law has increasingly become a competition factor. Taking the European experiences and the regulations of the harmonisation of laws into consideration, the harmony of corporate law with company law, the law on liquidation and final settlement and capital market law had to be established. Corporate law is a competition issue, where it is easy to lag behind, if we do not avail of the new technological instruments, or if we do not make the internal organisational order flexible.

In terms of the obligations of chief officers, the law establishes the institute of the so-called wrongful trading in order to, when close to bankruptcy, the management of the company be retained from assumption of risk at an unjustified level, prejudicing the interest of creditors. Subsequent to the occurrence of the situation threatening with the insolvency of the business association, the chief officers are obliged to perform their management duties based on the priority of the interests of the creditors of the company. In case of the material breach of this, the chief officer is obliged to assume responsibility towards the creditors.

For the sake of strengthening the responsible behaviour of the managing director, the solvency test was introduced. In accordance with the provisions of the memorandum of association, the managing director should make a declaration in memorandum of association, the managing director should make a declaration in writing on the fact that certain payments do not endanger the solvency of the company, and the enforcement of the interest of the creditors. The managing director assumes responsibility for:

- the damages caused by payments performed without making a declaration; or
- making an untruthful declaration in accordance with the general provisions relating to the chief officers.

The new regulation treats the cases when the member of the company performs the formal provision of assets not in accordance with the legal relationship with the limited liability company but looking for a civil law legal title, the provision of assets aims at the preference of the member to the creditors (concealed dividend) the same way as unlawful provision of assets.

The domestic share law was harmonised with the EU regulation on the protection of creditors. The shareholder can only receive assets in accordance with the conditions and the order of procedure included in the legal regulations, which cannot endanger the solvency and future reasonable management of the business of the stock corporation, and the solvency test ensures the reliable operation from the aspect of the protection of the creditors. In case of stock corporations operating on the regulated capital market, the legislator, by means of the regulation:

- ensures the legal protection of the shareholder investors; and
- improves the legal conditions of external market control.

The corporate law renewed in 2007 as well as the significantly modified and amended law on liquidation and final settlement were almost harmonised in order to ensure the appropriate enforcement of the interests of creditors.

Chapter 10

Inapplicability of the Provisions on Entailing Personal Liability in Insolvency Proceedings and Intervention of the Companies Act in Romania

Lavinia Iancu

Introduction[1]

This paper is intended to be a research of the legal Romanian provisions regarding the dissolving and the official receivership of the companies, both on the basis of 31/1990 - The Companies Law and 85/2006 – Insolvency Law, the tangential and intersection points of these two regulations and the problems encountered when put into practice.

The approach of this theme had, as a starting point, the substantial modification of the Companies Law 31/1990 through the 441/2006 Law and the coming into force of the new Insolvency Code, the 85/2006 Law, by abrogating the 64/1995 Law, both changes being initiated following the negative observations made by the European Commission competent in this field. Although the European Commission's observations were taken into consideration, in that were instituted new, simple and efficient proceedings, characterized by celerity, for the elimination from the economic circuit of the companies that, for various reasons could not stay on the Romanian market, when put into practice these proceeding have created and still create a lot of difficulties.

Domestic Procedures

The existing practical problems in the ways to dissolve and to liquidate the companies on the basis of the Companies Law could be synthesized as follows:

- The partners' possibility to expunge an indebted company, without any sanction being taken against them even if they have acted fraudulently and the transmission to the partners of the assets' property, assets that were taken out of the creditors legal proceedings;

[1] The author would like to thank Edwin Coe LLP for their sponsorship of the Academic Forum, which enabled the author to benefit from a travel grant to present this paper at the Barcelona Conference.

- The inexistence, in practice, of the certificate issued by the Commerce Register on the basis of which, at the same time with the erasure of the company, the real estate assets' property could be transmitted to the partners;
- The preferential mode in which the tax creditor is treated; and
- The complicated procedure of erasing from the market the companies that encounter financial difficulties.

Considering these problems we have concluded that there should be adopted a series of provisions from the Insolvency Law, reducing considerably in this manner the aforementioned problems.

The Inapplicability of the Personal Liability Provisions

The view of the author is that, at present, the 85/2006 Insolvency Law's provisions on entailing personal liability of the direction's members are inapplicable. The ineffectiveness stage of these provisions is of such extent that it profoundly affects the purpose itself of the Insolvency Law, "the payment of the debts to the creditors", since, preponderantly, the application of the personal liability procedure is the only method through which creditors can still recover debt. If the argument can be sustained for the adoption of certain provisions from the Insolvency Law, for the purpose of covering the deficiencies in the Companies Law, nonetheless there is also an obligation to recommend the taking into consideration of the Companies Law's provisions, because the already mentioned Insolvency Law's stipulations on entailing the personal liability are not applicable.

The conclusions of this paper are fully concordant with the European Commission's Report on Romanian Justice, presented in July 2008, where is stated that "the juridical and institutional framework is fragile and needs to be consolidated", "the reform of the judicial process is slowly advancing and the progresses are unequal", "the performance of the Romanian judicial system stumbles on the judicial insecurity caused by many factors, including the irregular application of the law". Also, the Report concerning the state of the Romanian Justice in 2007, released in July 2008, in which the Superior Council of the Romanian Magistrate, admits the fact that the trusting level of the population on the judicial system is one of the lowest among European Community member-states, and that the reform did not provide conclusive results.

Nevertheless, we consider that, during all the period pre and post adhesion at the European Community, the Romanian legal system has been profoundly and positively altered, the modifications being meant to align Romanian legislation to European standards. Considering this, the legislation seems to lack the non correlation of the legal provisions, while the impossible application of certain legal stipulations seems to be natural.

Chapter 11

Reconciling the European Capital Regime with Modern Insolvency Law: Experience from the Czech Reform

Tomáš Richter

Introduction

Insolvency changes the capital structure of a corporation dramatically: shareholders' equity is wiped out and the residual interest "moves" to creditors, who stand ahead of shareholders in the queue for the company's assets.[1]

This simple economic logic is, however, often not easily reconciled with legal rules governing the life (and, metaphorically, also the death) of corporations. In particular, with regard to European joint-stock companies (the PLCs, AGs, SAs and equivalents), the Second Company Law Directive (Directive 77/91/EEC, as amended) is completely oblivious of the aforementioned economic change and its implications for the financing and governance of the insolvent joint-stock corporation.

Any European legislator wishing to provide its market with an insolvency law reflecting basic economic logic of the corporation's capital structure will therefore face a dilemma of whether one can be Europe-compliant and make sense at the same time.[2] The Czech Parliament, when approving the new Czech Insolvency Act ("IA"),[3] was no exception. The lessons learnt in that process might well help other jurisdictions in and out of the European Union. I will therefore try to briefly summarise them in this paper.

---

[1] Of course, in non-trivial capital structures involving numerous layers of debt and potentially hybrid claims, working out who exactly the residual interest moves to is one of the most difficult issues in any market-based insolvency process, it is however not one with which I will deal with here (see e.g. L.M. LoPucki, "The Myth of the Residual Owner: An Empirical Study", UCLA School of Law, Law & Econ Research Paper No. 3-11 (2003)).

[2] The (Euro)sceptic might insist that this dilemma is by no means exclusive to the area of corporate insolvency.

[3] Act 182/2006 Coll., in force since 1 January 2008. An English translation of the Act (in its original 2006 version) is available in "The Act on Insolvency and Its Resolution", Aleš Čeněk, Plzeň, 2006, ISBN 80-86898-88-9.

Conflict Scenarios

The main areas of conflict between the logic of corporate insolvency and European corporate law are essentially three:
- the registered share capital regime and changes thereto;
- pre-emptive rights of current shareholders; and
- the (related) problem with disclosure under the Prospectus Directive (Directive 2003/71/EC).

I will discuss them in that order, with a short conclusion at the end of the paper.

The Registered Share Capital Regime and Changes thereto

Historically, the first conflict has not been a big issue in Europe. In traditional European bankruptcy law where liquidation of the company's assets and distribution of the proceeds among the creditors was basically the only option, the rules on changes of registered capital (or, indeed, any other rules of corporate law) did not matter much. After the bankruptcy dividend was paid out to creditors, the company died its sad death by being struck off the commercial register, and none of the rules of the Second Company Law Directive ever came in play.

However, as soon as one starts to think in terms of non-liquidation proceedings (termed usually "reorganization" after the US model),[4] the picture changes quite dramatically. Here, the insolvent company's assets traditionally remain in the left-hand side of the original balance sheet while the right-hand side is reconstructed such that the balance sheet gets "back in balance".[5] At bottom, given that assets stay where they are, the ways in which the balance sheet can be fixed are not that numerous, really. One can either reduce (or reschedule or do something else with) the debt, or inject new equity. One can of course do both at the same time by swapping debt for equity, which is done frequently when insolvent (or near insolvent) companies are recapitalised.[6] In any jurisdiction that follows the concept of a fixed registered share capital (such as the Czech

---

[4] The most recent self-contained treatment that I am aware of is E. Warren, Chapter 11: Reorganizing American Businesses (Essentials), Aspen Publishers, New York, 2008.

[5] History may of course prove me wrong but for now, I assume that the trend of the past 10 to 15 years in which U.S. market practice essentially turned Chapter 11 into liquidation proceedings conducted by a "private trustee" (the chief restructuring officer) on behalf of the main creditors (see e.g. D.G. Baird and R.K. Rasmussen, "The End of Bankruptcy", University of Chicago, The Law School, John M. Olin Law & Economics Working Paper No. 173 (2002); D.G. Baird and R.K. Rasmussen, "Chapter 11 at Twilight", University of Chicago, The Law School, John M. Olin Law & Economics Working Paper No. 201 (2003)) will reverse itself as the result of the dramatic drop in the supply of credit available to private equity and other buyers that we have been observing since the beginning of the financial crisis in summer 2007 and that is likely to continue for some time in the future, if not forever. In an environment in which buyers cannot raise funding quickly and cheaply, "traditional" non-liquidation proceedings (such as Chapter 11 in its original shape prior to the market metamorphosis) regain their importance in preserving the value of productive assets in times of crisis.

[6] In Czech corporate law, this would mechanically be achieved by the company issuing the new shares to creditors "for cash" with the creditors setting their obligation to pay the issue price off against the debts owing to them from the company. (S. 59(8) of the Czech Commercial Code, Act 513/1991, as amended).

Republic),[7] issuance of new shares by definition means a change (an increase) of the registered capital.

Increase in the Registered Share Capital

And this is where the problem starts. For under Article 25 of the Second Company Law Directive, any increase in [the share] capital must be decided upon by the general meeting (i.e. the shareholders), the directive making no exception for insolvent companies. This, however, is inconsistent with the economic logic of insolvency: giving shareholders of an insolvent company (i.e. investors whose interest in the company has been erased in economic terms) the right to decide about its new capital structure amounts (or at least may amount) to giving them a veto over the reorganization proceedings. Such veto can be very valuable in the shareholders' hands because it can be used to extract value from senior claimants (creditors) by way of hold-up.

Mindful of this logic, the Czech Insolvency Act provides that in insolvency proceedings, the decision-making powers of the general meeting are suspended during reorganization proceedings (section 333 (1) of the IA).[8] Those powers are vested in the trustee, who is initially appointed by the insolvency court and may later, when claims filed in the proceedings are verified, be replaced by creditors' vote (sections 25 and 29 of the IA). The one-off decision on the new capital structure will likely not be made by the trustee but rather decided upon as part of the reorganization plan (section 341 (1) of the IA), which must, in principle, be approved by all creditor classes (section 347 of the IA).

The question is whether this solution, economically sound as it may be, complies with the Second Company Law Directive or not.

I believe that there are two principal reasons to think that it does. Firstly, under section 335 of the IA, shareholders are treated as creditors in reorganization, with the right to vote on the reorganization plan (including a plan involving the increase of share capital) in a separate class (section 337 (2) (b) of the IA). In their class, they vote by a 2/3rds majority of capital and a simple majority of members, the former requirement being consistent with the majority requirement of Article 40 of the Second Company Law Directive. Hence, if the shareholder class votes for the plan, Article 25 can be said to have been substantively complied with, even though, as a matter of form, the shareholder congregation was not called a "general meeting" but rather a class vote in a creditors' meeting.

The more interesting situation would arise if the shareholder class voted against the plan. In such case, under the IA, the Czech bankruptcy court could still approve the plan (subject to other conditions) if at least one of the creditor classes

---

[7] S. 154(1) and S. 202 ff. of the Czech Commercial Code.

[8] The one exception is the right to elect the directors, which the shareholders retain (S. 333(2) IA). The logic behind this slightly odd provision is to serve as the "carrot" that should entice directors to commence proceedings timely rather than hold out until the last moment out of fear of being replaced by the creditors. The "stick" is directors' liability to creditors for late filing (timeliness is measured against both the cash-flow and the balance sheet test of insolvency, S. 3 IA) where the damages are presumed equal to the creditors' shortfall suffered in the insolvency proceedings (S. 99(2) IA).

senior to the shareholders that is not getting the full present value of its claims under the plan[9] voted for the plan.

Again, this is arguably a sound rule, but what of Article 25? Well, owing mainly to Greece, Article 25 has been tested in the European Court of Justice ("ECJ") a number of times. [10] On my reading, these judgments actually support the conclusion that an *increase of registered capital and the issuance of new shares without the approval of the company's shareholders do not violate Article 25 if effected inside insolvency proceedings.* This is because the ECJ, holding against various Greek governmental agencies who attempted to recapitalize Greek companies through governmental action without shareholders approval, rightly described those attempts as "ordinary reorganization measures" (*Pafitis*, at 57 and 58), "straightforward rationalization measure[s]" (*Syndesmos Melon*, at 27 and 28) or "straightforward rejuvenation measure[s]" (*Karella*, at 30). In *Pafitis*, the ECJ expressly distinguished these measures from "execution […] or liquidation measure[s]"(at 58). In all of the cited decisions, the ECJ admitted that the Second Company Law Directive does not prevent the taking of execution and liquidation measures, putting the company in a regime of forced liquidation for the protection of the rights of its creditors (*Pafitis* at 57; *Syndesmos Melon* at 27; *Karella* at 30). According to the ECJ, the Directive shall apply for as long as the company's members and its normal organs were not stripped of their powers, i.e. *for as long as the company exists in its own structures* (*Syndesmos Melon* at 27 and 28; *Karella* at 30, emphasis added).

I think that the last test is the key to the present analysis. Although, viewed through the terminology of modern insolvency law, the ECJ referred to the relevant proceeding bit inaptly as "execution […] or liquidation measure[s]" taken for the protection of creditors' rights, there can be no doubt, in my opinion, that what it really had in mind are insolvency proceedings.

Applying the ECJ's criteria in the context of Czech insolvency law, I find it quite compelling to conclude that a company declared insolvent and put into reorganization proceedings by a court under the IA no longer exists in its own structures. Its shareholders were stripped off their decision-making powers; the board stays in place but not under the powers conferred by corporate law but rather as an agent of the company in its capacity as the debtor-in-possession (section 2(g) of the IA). The board is in fact in the position of the insolvency trustee (sections 36 and 330(1) of the IA) and exercises its rights for the benefit of the creditors, under

---

[9] That there will be at least one such "impaired" class is almost self-evident given that the company must be insolvent or at least threatened by insolvency to be able to commence insolvency proceedings in the first place (S. 1(a) and 3 IA).

[10] See e.g. ECJ judgments C-367/96, Alexandros Kefalas and Others v Elliniko Dimosio (Greek State) and Organismos Oikonomikis Anasygkrotisis Epicheiriseon AE (OAE) of 12 May 1998; C-441/93, Panagis Pafitis and others v Trapeza Kentrikis Ellados A.E. and others of 12 March 1996 ("Pafitis"); C-381/89, Syndesmos Melon tis Eleftheras Evangelikis Ekklissias and others v Greek State and others of 24 March 1992 ("Syndesmos Melon"); C-134/91 a C-135/91, Kerafina-Keramische-und Finanz Holding AG and Vioktimatiki AEVE v Hellenic Republic and Organismos Oikonomikis Anasygkrotissis Epicheirisseon AE of 12 November 1992; C-19/90 and C 20-90, Marina Karella and Nicolas Karellas v Minister for Industry, Energy and Technology and Organismos Anasygkrotiseos Epicheiriseon AE of 30 May 1991 ("Karella").

the supervision of the trustee, the creditors' committee and the court. Whether and in what form the company will exist in the future is decided by the creditors or the court, not the shareholders.

It follows from the above, I think, that Article 25 can not and does not apply to companies in formal insolvency proceedings as defined in current European law in the European Insolvency Regulation (Regulation (EC) 1346/2000, Annex A). This in spite of the fact that the Second Company Law Directive does not expressly state so-perhaps because at the time it was drafted, no one in the then-EEC could imagine a different type of insolvency proceedings than straightforward liquidation and because the drafters dealing with the subsequent amendments of the Directive (most recently and most notably through Directive 2006/68/EC whose implementation in the Czech Republic was still pending as of the time of writing) were busy enough fixing all the other antiquities and inefficiencies of the Directive.

Decrease in the Registered Share Capital

So far, I have only discussed instances when, typically in return for the cancellation of debt, the reorganized company issues new shares and hence increases its registered share capital.

However, reorganization proceedings may also bring about situations involving the reduction of the registered share capital. Apart from instances where this is undertaken through consensus of all classes, including the shareholders, there may be situations in which the reduction of the current share capital is a necessity dictated by the logic of insolvency law. Most notably, such need may arise where the reorganization plan is to be approved by the court over the objection of a creditor class, a process casually referred to as the *cram-down*.[11]

The economic driver behind this is usually referred to as the *absolute priority rule*, in other words, the basic principle that the ranking of investors' claims on the company's assets (or, in other words, the relative value of those claims) as it follows from non-insolvency law must be observed inside insolvency as well, unless a different rule is dictated by the very nature of the insolvency proceedings.[12] Applied in our context, the absolute priority rule requires that where a reorganization plan is to be approved by a court over the objection of a class that is not receiving the full present value of its claims, the court asked to *cram-down* the plan on the objecting class must be satisfied that no class junior to the objecting class is receiving (or keeping) any value under the plan at all.[13] Thus, if a reorganization plan were to be approved by the court over the objection of a class of, say, general or subordinated creditors, the court could only approve the plan if

---

[11] See e.g. E. Warren and J. Westbrook, The Law of Debtors and Creditors, Text, Cases, and Problems, Aspen Publishers, New York, 2006, p. 655 ff.

[12] This is one of the main insights bestowed on us once and for all by Thomas Jackson in his The Logic and Limits of Bankruptcy Law, Harvard University Press, Cambridge (MA), 1986, reprint Beard Books, Washington, D.C., 2001.

[13] E. Warren and J. Westbrook, supra under 11, p. 656. The Czech Insolvency Act's rule of absolute priority, drawing heavily on the U.S. model, is contained in ss. 348(2) and 349 IA.

current shareholders are wiped out completely by the plan, i.e. if they are stripped off their shares in the company.[14]

In regimes of fixed registered share capital, such "wiping out" by definition involves:

- reducing the previous registered share capital down to zero; and
- equipping the company with new registered share capital (in the minimum amount required by the law[15]).

Luckily, reducing the registered share capital inside insolvency proceedings presents a smaller interpretation challenge than increasing it. This is because Article 30 of the Second Company Law Directive that requires a reduction in the registered share capital to be decided upon by the general meeting contains and explicit exemption for reductions conducted "under a court order". Because any reorganization plan under the Czech Insolvency Act (whether or not approved by all classes) must also be approved by the insolvency court to take effect (sections 348-349 of the IA), one can simply rely on this "under a court order" exemption. One can therefore safely conclude that European company allows reductions of registered share capital inside insolvency proceedings otherwise than with the consent of the shareholders provided that such reductions are approved by the insolvency court. Giving the hold-up problem that a different rule would create (see the argument in part 1.1 above), this is a welcome conclusion.

Unfortunately, the enquiry into the Second Company Law Directive's effects within non-liquidation insolvency proceedings does not end quite yet. The remaining topic that must be dealt with is shareholders' pre-emptive rights.

Pre-Emptive Rights of Current Shareholders

Closely related to Article 25 is Article 29 of the Second Company Law Directive, under which whenever the [share] capital of a joint-stock company is increased by consideration in cash, the shares must be offered on pre-emptive basis to shareholders in proportion to the capital represented by their shares. The Directive provides for several exemptions from this rule (e.g. Articles 29(2) and 41), however, none of them applies to insolvency of the company.

Interestingly, most of the ECJ case law cited above in relation to Article 25 does not help in relation to Article 29 – this is because in the majority of the Greek government's interventions in the capital structures of the distressed companies that lead to the litigation, pre-emptive rights of current shareholders over the newly issued shares were observed. The one exception was the Syndesmos Melon case where the relevant Greek minister decided, under the administrative powers granted by special national legislation, to increase the company's share capital via a debt/equity swap in which the pre-emptive rights of current

---

[14] Where the objecting class is the shareholder class itself, the court may cram-down the plan on it if at least one class of unsecured creditors is receiving less under the plan than the full present value of the principal amount of their claims and of interest accruing thereon up to the date on which the plan takes effect (S. 349(4) IA).

[15] The Second Company Law Directive currently requires in Article 6 that this amount be not less than Euro 25,000 or equivalent in member state currency.

The Intersection of Insolvency and Company Laws

shareholders would be disapplied. In that case, the ECJ held (*Syndesmos Melon* at 33 and 37) that the disapplication of shareholders' pre-emptive rights via governmental action violated Article 29 of the Second Company Law Directive. At the same time, however, the ECJ also observed that that finding does not mean that Community law precludes the Member States from derogating from those provisions *whatever the circumstances* (ditto, at 34, emphasis added). The ECJ went on to cite the express exemptions in Articles 19, 41, 42 and 43 of the Directive by way of example. More importantly, however, in deciding Syndesmos Melon, the ECJ expressly relied on its earlier case law (esp. *Karella*), reiterating that *"[w]hilst the directive does not preclude the taking of execution measures and, in particular, liquidation measure placing the company under compulsory liquidation in the interests of safeguarding creditors' rights, it nevertheless continues to apply as long as the company's shareholders and normal bodies have not been divested of their powers"* (*Syndesmos Melon* at 27, emphasis added).

Once again, I think that this test contains the ultimate answer to the present enquiry. As I have argued in relation to Article 25 of the Second Company Law Directive above, a company that is being reorganized inside insolvency proceedings such as those under the Czech Insolvency Act is a company whose shareholders and normal bodies have been divested of their powers. In the other way the ECJ phrases the same concept, such company no longer continues within its own structures (Syndesmos Melon at 28, emphasis added). I therefore conclude that the Article 29 pre-emptive rights need not be applied by companies in insolvency proceedings under the European Insolvency Regulation.

The above-mentioned argument applies equally to consensual reorganization, i.e. proceedings where the reorganization plan is agreed by all classes, as well as non-consensual reorganization, i.e. proceedings in which the reorganization plan is being adopted by the court over the objection of a class. In the latter case, however, there are two more arguments that should be mentioned for the sake of completeness. The first is rather technical, the second is more fundamental in its economic logic.

Firstly, where the current registered share capital is being "wiped out" as a pre-condition for the approval of the plan, i.e. the current registered capital is first reduced to zero, the old shareholders' shares actually do not exist as a matter of law at the moment the company's capital is then increased again. Technically speaking, the old shareholders have no shares in the company any longer (although, as a matter of fact, they may of course still hold pieces of paper or electronic entries called "a share") – hence, they are not shareholders and do not enjoy any pre-emptive rights at all.

Secondly, and more fundamentally, the pre-emptive right to subscribe newly issued shares is an option and each option has its value. Since that option pertains to the shareholders under their original investment in the company's shares, keeping it arguably means keeping a valuable claim on the company's assets. However, if the reorganization plan is crammed-down on a class senior to the shareholders that is not getting the full present value of its claim, we know that the absolute priority rule requires that the shareholders receive (and retain) no value in the reorganized capital structure of the company whatsoever. Under this logic, the original shareholders may not be entitled to exercise the pre-emptive rights pertaining to their old shares over any new shares issued by the company under the reorganization plan. If they did, the court could not approve the plan over the objection of another, more senior class.[16]

For the avoidance of doubt – none of the above is meant to suggest that old shareholders may not participate in the new capital structure of the reorganized company *where all senior classes agree with such arrangement*. However, where there is no agreement among all classes and the court is called upon to cram the plan down, my conclusion is that Article 29 of the Second Company Law Directive does not preclude a national insolvency court from approving a reorganization plan under which the old shareholders have no right to acquire newly issued shares on the basis of the pre-emptive rights pertaining to their old shares in the company.

Disclosure under the Prospectus Directive

The Prospectus Directive (2003/71/EC) is a measure aimed at harmonising the disclosure requirements upon public offerings or listings of securities within the EU. For that purpose, the Directive contains a EU-wide definition of a public offer (Article 2(1)(d)), as well as a list of exemptions from the obligation to publish a prospectus upon a public offer (Article 4).

Unfortunately, none of the exemptions in Article 4 seems to cover the situation in which securities are offered in non-liquidation insolvency proceedings under a reorganization plan, whether or not there are special disclosure requirements set out in the insolvency legislation and whether or not such disclosures are approved by the insolvency court.[17] This seems weird, especially given that Article 4 contains specific exemptions, inter alia, for securities issued in the context of tender offers or mergers, provided that a disclosure document is available in connection with the said transactions containing, in the opinion of the national authority empowered to review such document, information equivalent to that of a prospectus (Articles 4(1)(b) and (c)).

In the context of reorganization proceedings under the Czech Insolvency Act, the reorganization plan must be accompanied by a detailed disclosure report approved by the insolvency court (section 343 of the IA).[18] Under these circumstances, it seems completely unnecessary to burden the reorganized company with the obligation to produce an have approved with a different regulator a separate prospectus.

I therefore suggest that the European legislator amends Article 4 of the Prospectus Directive such that it contains an appropriate exemption for securities issued in connection with insolvency proceedings, similar to the exemptions currently available in Articles 4(1)(b) and (c). The fact the such exemption is

---

[16] This argument is in line with the majority opinion in the U.S. Supreme Court case of *Bank of America National Trust & Savings Association v. 203 North LaSalle Street Partnership* 526 U.S. 434 (1999), discussed e.g. in E. Warren and J. Westbrook, supra under 11, p. 657 ff.

[17] An example of such exemption can be found in S. 1145 of the U.S. Bankruptcy Code.

[18] The structure and the details of the report are prescribed in the Annex to Ministry of Justice Regulation No. 311/2007.

The Intersection of Insolvency and Company Laws

missing in European legislation dating as recently as from 2003 may serve as a reminder of how long a journey lies ahead of us in Europe before we get accustomed to the idea that corporate insolvency may amount to more than, or indeed something totally different from, the selling of the company's assets and distributing the proceeds to creditors.

Conclusion

In this article, I have reviewed the Second Company Law Directive for compatibility with non-liquidation insolvency proceedings and found it wanting in many respects.

On its face, the Directive's Article 25 (and to an extent also Article 29) suggests that European company law simply precludes recapitalization of European joint-stock companies in reorganization proceedings.

Luckily enough, on careful reading, the ECJ case law on the Directive can be used to reach the opposite, economically sensible conclusion. This is what I have primarily tried to do in the article.

The situation with the Prospectus Directive is less satisfactory, I am afraid, as no amount of careful reading will result in a conclusion that the reorganizing company will not be forced to draw up and have approved a prospectus if it makes a public offer of securities as part of the reorganization proceedings. This is result is unfortunate and I suggested that the Directive should be amended such that reorganizing companies are not burdened with double disclosure exercises in instances where they are already making sufficient disclosures under national insolvency law rules.

PART IV
THE EDWIN COE LECTURE

The Academic Forum would like to thank its sponsors Edwin Coe LLP
for enabling the delivery of this lecture at the Barcelona Conference.

2 Stone Buildings, Lincoln's Inn, London WC2A 3TH
T: +44 (0) 20 7691 4000 F: +44 (0) 20 7691 4111
W: www.edwincoe.com

Chapter 12

The Present and Future
of Multinational Insolvency

Jay L. Westbrook

I – Current Issues

Introduction

Among the multitude of issues currently being litigated in the field of multinational insolvency, the following five broad areas stand out as the most important to discuss:

- the Model Law on Cross-Border Insolvency;
- choice of law;
- discharge or enforcement of bankruptcy judgments;
- denationalized bankruptcy; and
- corporate groups.

The Model Law on Cross-Border Insolvency

Since the adoption of the Model Law on Cross-Border Insolvency, the most intense litigation has been with regard to recognition of a foreign proceeding as a main or non-main proceeding. A two-sided rule may be emerging: an insolvency proceeding will not receive recognition and assistance as a main proceeding if it is brought in a jurisdiction with little or no economic relationship to the debtor, whereas a business that actually relocates its most important economic or administrative functions to a new jurisdiction may be allowed to enjoy whatever legal benefits that move might provide if it then files for insolvency.

The rule against recognition of proceedings from jurisdictions with minimum connections with the debtor is found in the *In re Bear Stearns*[1] case from the United States and the *Eurofood* case[2] from the European Court of Justice. Although the debtors in Bear were incorporated in the Cayman Islands, the court

---

* I am grateful to Jessica Bennett, Texas '09, for expert research assistance. I must claim any remaining errors.

[1] In re Bear Stearns High-Grade Structured Credit Strategies Master Fund, Ltd., 374 B.R. 122 (Bankr. S.D.N.Y. 2007).

[2] Bondi v. Bank of America, N.A. (In re Eurofood IFSC Ltd.) [2006] ECR I-3813, p. 18-19, 35, 2006 WL 1142304 (ECJ 2 May 2006).

ruled that the Cayman proceedings could not be recognized as either main or non-main proceedings because the debtors had too little real contact with the islands for them to constitute the "centre of main interests" ("COMI") and therefore the home of the primary insolvency proceedings. The court further ruled that naked incorporation was not enough even to permit recognition as a non-main proceeding.[3] In *Eurofood*, the European Court of Justice similarly stated that a "letter box" presence was insufficient to make a jurisdiction eligible for hosting a primary proceeding. Thus, it appears that remote jurisdictions will not be entitled to receive recognition under either the Model Law or the European Regulation.

Recent articles have supported a "third way" process for recognition, beyond recognition as a main or non-main proceeding under the Model Law.[4] Given that the fact that non-recognition as an insolvency proceeding merely precludes the granting of relief under the Model Law but does not preclude extension of cooperation short of that,[5] it is not entirely clear what difficulty their authors seek to avoid.

On the other side of things, recent European decisions suggest that a company that actually relocates its principal office to another jurisdiction may thereby make that jurisdiction its COMI for a subsequent insolvency filing.[6]

Although the Model Law has been operating successfully in a number of countries,[7] it is disappointing that some jurisdictions, such as Germany[8] and Spain,[9] have recently reformed their laws without adopting the Model Law,

---

[3] A similar result was reached by another Southern District judge. *In re Basis Yield Alpha Fund (Master)*, 381 B.R. 37, 46-47 (S.D.N.Y. 2007) ("In this case, genuine issues of material fact exist as to the location of Basis Yield's COMI. While the Court does not in any way rule out the possibility that facts could be adduced at an evidentiary hearing sufficient to make a case for entitlement to recognition, the JPLs are not now entitled to recognition as a matter of law.").

[4] A. Ranney-Marinelli, "Overview of Chapter 15 Ancillary and Other Cross-Border Cases", 82 AM. BANKR. L.J. 269, 303 (2008) ("[A] third approach is to interpret § 1509(f) broadly, permitting many types of relief to fall under the rubric of 'collecting or recovering a claim which is property of the debtor," so that Chapter 15 recognition is not required."); D.P. Stromes, "The Extraterritorial Reach of the Bankruptcy Code's Automatic Stay: Theory vs. Practice", 33 BROOK. J. INT'L L. 277 (2007); J. Pottow, "The Myth (and Realities) of Forum Shopping in Transnational Insolvency", 32 BROOK. J. INT'L L. 785 (2007).

[5] 11 U.S.C. §§15, 25-27.

[6] *Official Receiver v. Eichler* [2007] BPIR 1636 14, 16 (Chan. Div.) (noting the right of a debtor to change his centre of main interests); *Shierson v. Vlieland-Boddy* [2005] EWCA Civ 974 55 (Ct. of App. Civ. Div.).

[7] For United States Chapter 15 cases, see www.chapter15.com.

[8] E. BRAUN, COMMENTARY ON THE GERMAN INSOLVENCY CODE 69 (2006); Nadine Farid, "The Fate of Intellectual Property Assets in Cross-Border Insolvency Proceedings", 44 GONZ. L. REV. 39 (2008); B. Wessels, "Mutual Trust, Comity, and Respect Among States in International Insolvency Matters", Part II § 1 ¶8 (W.J. Norton, Jr. ed., 2005); J. Greene, "Bankruptcy Beyond Borders: Recognizing Foreign Proceedings in Cross-Border Insolvencies", 30 BROOK. J. INT'L L. 685, 724 (2005); C. Farley, "An Overview, Survey, and Critique of Administering Cross-Border Insolvencies", 27 HOUS. J. INT'L L. 181, 206 (2004); A. Heidbrink, "The New German Rules on International Insolvency Law", 22-9 AM. BANKR. L.J. 16 (2003); J.M. Goffman and E.A. Michael, "Cross Border Insolvencies: A Comparative Examination of Insolvency Laws of Industrialized Countries", 12 J. Bankr. L. & Prac. 5 Art. 1 (2003).

[9] J.L. Westbrook, "Chapter 15 At Last", 79 AM. BANKR. L.J. 713, 721 (2005) ("The primary disappointment to date has been the failure of Germany and Spain to adopt the Model Law despite having enacted some new international provisions."); but see E. Bruce Leonard, "The International Scene: The International Year

---

The Intersection of Insolvency and Company Laws

resulting in only general provisions to guide their courts in cooperating with countries outside the "EU club."

Choice of Law

Three elements in choice-of-law deserve special attention: the dichotomous analysis of insolvency and non-insolvency law; choice-of-law issues in application of the avoiding powers; and the interaction of choice of law and choice of forum.

Generally: Two Choices

The choice-of-law analysis in insolvency is two-sided. One part concerns the law that created and governed a contract or property right prior to bankruptcy ("non-insolvency law"), such as a counterparty's entitlement to a contract claim against the insolvent business, while the other identifies the insolvency law that will govern its treatment in the insolvency proceeding, such as the enforceability of the contract claim and the fixing of the amount actually to be paid.

However, the cases often reflect a confusion of the two elements, as if the court believes that one law will govern both aspects of the claim. A classic example is the *Lernout* case in the United States and Belgium.[10] The lower courts failed to see that two different choice-of-law questions were presented under the differing priority rules in the two countries – one of non-insolvency law and one of insolvency law.

Once an issue has been identified as governed by insolvency law, the next step is the identification of the applicable insolvency law. I suggest a general rule

in Review", 22-10 AM. BANKR. INST. J. 22, 78 (2003-2004) ("Legislation also has been passed in Spain that is to become effective in 2004; it has international insolvency provisions that parallel, and in fact, may be more extensive than those in the model law, but that also reflect the EU Regulation on Insolvency Proceedings."); A. Mechele Dickerson, "Conference on Sovereign Debt Restructuring: The view from the Legal Academy: A Politically Viable Approach to Sovereign Debt Restructuring", 53 EMORY L.J. 997, 1041 ("Only Mexico appears to have fully embraced and implemented principles contained in the UNCITRAL Model Law in enacting domestic insolvency legislation [whereas]…Spain ha[s] adopted legislation that contains many of the principles of the Model Law."). The United Nations Commission on International Trade Law (UNCITRAL) does not list Spain as an adopting country: www.uncitral.org/uncitral/en/uncitral_texts/insolvency/1997Model_status.html.

[10] *Lernout & Hauspie Speech Products N.V. v. Stonington Partners, Inc.*, 268 B.R. 395 (D. Del. 2001), rev'd, 310 F.3d 118 (3d Cir. 2002), on remand *In re Lernout & Hauspie Speech Products N.V.*, 301 B.R. 651 (Bankr. D. Del. 2003). See J.L. Westbrook, "Universalism and Choice of Law", 23 PENN. ST. INT'L L. REV. 625 (2005) (discusses Lernout at length); J.L. Westbrook, "International Judicial Negotiation", 38 TEX. INT'L L.J. 567 (2003) (refers to Lernout in footnotes); J. Pottow, "Greed and Pride in International Bankruptcy: The Problems of and Proposed Solutions to 'Local Interests'", 104 MICH. L. REV. 1899 (2006) (discusses Lernout); L. Salafia, "Cross-Border Insolvency in the United States and its Application to Multinational Corporate Groups", 21 CONN. J. INT'L L. 297, 332 (2006) (discusses Lernout); K.J. Beckering, "United States Cross-Border Corporate Insolvency: The Impact of Chapter 15 on Comity and the New Legal Environment", 14 LAW & BUS. REV. AM. 281, 308-309 (2008) (refers to Lernout in footnote); L.M. Lopucki, "Global and Out of Control?", 79 AM. BANKR. L.J. 79, 92 (2005) (discusses Lernout); J. Pottow, "Procedural Incrementalism: A Model for International Bankruptcy", 45 VA. J. INT'L L. 935 (2005) (discusses Lernout in footnotes).

applying the law of the primary proceeding on a global basis, with exceptions for local claims of employees, suppliers, and tort claimants whose expectations of local law application should be vindicated.[11]

Avoidance (Paulian) Actions

Two considerations should dominate choice of law for avoidance: a realistic concern for predictability and the connection between avoidance and distribution.

Predictability is important where the substantial differences among national laws create expensive uncertainty in multinational transactions. On the other hand, there are real limits on the extent to which predictability is obtainable.[12]

The second element is the relationship between avoidance and distribution. All avoiding powers require a balance between two policy objectives. The avoidance of fraud and achievement of distribution equality among creditors of equal rank[13] must be balanced against the threat every avoidance poses to the stability of commercial transactions.[14]

Given countries' differing avoidance policies and distribution priorities, the choice of applicable avoidance law should depend on which proceeding will be distributing the proceeds of an avoidance recovery.[15] In a universalist system, that will mean the primary proceeding. In a territorialist system, that will mean each country that opens a proceeding and permits an attack on the transaction.[16] Some might propose a middle solution where the choice-of-law rule would be the situs of the transaction. However, even if one can identify *the* place of the transaction, in many cases the situs chosen by the parties would be a law that would *not* permit avoidance.

The Interaction Between Choice of Law and Choice of Forum

Finally, the HIH case exemplifies the third key to choice-of-law decisions.[17] HIH, an Australian company with substantial assets in the United Kingdom, entered

[11] As to choice of labour law, for example, see J.L. Westbrook, "Multinational Financial Distress: The Last Hurrah of Territorialism", 41 Tex. Int'l L.J. 321 (2006) (reviewing L.M. LOPUCKI, COURTING FAILURE: HOW COMPETITION FOR BIG CASES IS CORRUPTING THE BANKRUPTCY COURTS (2005)).

[12] For example, in the COMI context, I have argued that "too exclusive a focus on predictability is…a mistake, especially if it leads to a rule that would choose legal 'havens' as COMIs."). J.L. Westbrook, "Locating the Eye of the Financial Storm", 32 BROOK. J. INT'L L. 1019, 1028 (2007).

[13] This factor is further supported in some countries, like the United States, by a desire to provide comfort to creditors in a workout situation that an effort by other creditors to steal a march during negotiations will be set aside if an insolvency proceeding is brought. Thus the avoiding powers can serve as an important support for a stand still agreement, especially if not all creditors have agreed.

[14] The adverse effect on other commercial transactions is no doubt lower in avoiding a transaction that is fraudulent in fact, because parties know that such transactions are legally vulnerable.

[15] J.L. Westbrook, "Avoidance of Pre-Bankruptcy Transactions in Multinational Bankruptcy Cases", 42 TEX. INT'L L. J. 899 (2007).

[16] One of the numerous difficulties with a territorialist system is that the transaction might be attacked by liquidators from several jurisdictions with plausible connections to the transaction, resulting in inconsistent results and perhaps multiple recoveries.

[17] McGrath v. Riddell [2008] UKHL 21 ("HIH").

insolvency proceedings in Australia. A provisional liquidation was opened in England. The two jurisdictions had different priority rules.[18] The lower courts decided they were bound by the English priority rules and therefore could not release the assets to Australia. The House of Lords held the assets could be released, but sharply split as to the rationale for the result.

The Australian court's request enjoyed the benefit of the United Kingdom Insolvency Act,[19] which permits English courts to cooperate fully with courts from countries like Australia designated by the government under section 426. On that basis, two of the five judges resolved the problem by holding that section 426 permitted them to choose to apply Australian law. However, Lord Hoffmann and another judge adopted a choice-of-forum approach, holding that English common law permitted the English court to act in an ancillary role and to turn over assets to the primary court as part of a long-standing commitment to a universalist approach, quite apart from the impact of section 426. The fifth judge accepted section 426 as resolving the issue in the case, but did not take a position as to the universalism theory. Thus in a case from a jurisdiction not covered by section 426 (for example, the United States) the vote of this panel would be two no, two yes, and one unknown.

Discharge and Enforcement

The effect of discharge becomes important in corporate cases where the effectiveness of a reorganization plan or scheme is dependent upon the recognition and enforcement of the court orders approving the plan by the courts in other jurisdictions.

According to the Principles adopted in the Transnational Insolvency Project of the American Law Institute (ALI),[20] a party should be bound by the plan if it asserts a claim, if it otherwise seeks to benefit from a reorganization proceeding or to influence its outcome,[21] or if it accepts payment under the plan[22].

[18] HIH, [2008] UKHL 21. 51.

[19] United Kingdom Insolvency Act, 2000, c. 39, § 14 (Eng.); United Kingdom Insolvency Act, 1986, c. 45, § 426 (Eng.).

[20] AM. LAW INST., PRINCIPLES OF COOPERATION AMONG THE NAFTA COUNTRIES 86-88 (2003) [hereafter "Principles"].

[21] Id. at 84 ("The key to reorganization law in each of the three NAFTA countries is the ability to bind interested parties to an agreed and approved plan. Not only must those who have agreed to be held to their agreement, but dissenters who have been outvoted by the legally required majorities must also be bound."); RESTATEMENT (THIRD) OF FOREIGN RELATIONS LAW: FOREIGN JUDGMENTS AND AWARDS, § 481 (1987) ("[A] final judgment of a court of a foreign state granting or denying recovery of a sum of money, establishing or confirming the status of a person, or determining interests in property, is conclusive between the parties, and is entitled to recognition in courts in the United States."); RESTATEMENT (SECOND) OF CONFLICT OF LAWS: RECOGNITION OF FOREIGN NATION JUDGMENTS § 98 (1971) ("Judgments rendered in a foreign nation…will be accorded the same degree of recognition to which sister State judgments are entitled. This is because the public interest requires that there be an end of litigation." See Baldwin v. Iowa State Traveling Men's Association, 283 U.S. 522, 525 (1931). A foreign nation judgment will be recognized in the American court where "there has been opportunity for a full and fair trial abroad before a court of competent jurisdiction." See Hilton v. Guyot, 159 U.S. 113, 202 (1895)); 18 C.A. WRIGHT, A.R. MILLER AND E.H. COOPER, FEDERAL PRACTICE AND PROCEDURE § 4404 (4th ed. 2008) ("A res judicata ruling by a court in another country also commands respect as itself res judicata, although without the compulsion of full faith and credit or federal supremacy.").

[22] Principles, supra note 20, at 88 (specifically, illustration 2).

Furthermore, a judgment should be binding if the court had proper international jurisdiction and the claimant had notice and a fair opportunity to be heard.[23] Otherwise, a reorganization plan should have no binding effect for a creditor that did not have sufficient connection with the jurisdiction approving the plan to justify jurisdiction in an ordinary civil suit involving the same or a closely related subject matter.

An example of discharge issues in multinational reorganizations is found in the cases where British insurance companies used the administration procedure in Britain to "run off" insurance obligations. Because these run offs often affect a large number of United States policyholders, these companies have come to the United States to obtain United States recognition of their run off schemes.[24] Despite a cogent attack on these schemes, at least four cases have already approved them under Chapter 15.[25]

Denationalized Insolvency Proceedings

A "denationalized" insolvency may result where a forum court has two characteristics: it is prepared to accept an insolvency filing from a corporation that has only a limited connection with the forum jurisdiction and it applies its own insolvency law to all insolvency issues.

Jurisdictions possessing these legal characteristics could attract filings, and the accompanying fees, by adopting insolvency laws pleasing to the debtors that decide where to file the proceedings.[26] The result may be a "denationalized"

[23] See Principles, supra note 20, at 88 (specifically, Procedural Principle 27).

[24] See generally, S.P. Johnston, "Why U.S. Courts Should Deny or Severely Condition Recognition to Schemes of Arrangement For Solvent Insurance Companies", 16 J. BANKR. L. PRAC. 6 Art. 2, 1 (2007).

[25] See Lion City Run-Off Private Limited, Case No. 06-B-10461 (Bankr. S.D.N.Y. 13 April 2006); In re Gordian Run-Off (UK) Ltd., Case No. 06-11563 (Bankr. S.D.N.Y. 28 August 2006); In re Europaische Ruckversicherungs-Gesellschaft in Zurich (European Reinsurance Company of Zurich), Case No. 06-13061 (Bankr. S.D.N.Y. 22 January 2007); In re Lloyd, No. 05-60100, 2005 Bankr. LEXIS 2794 (Bankr. S.D.N.Y. 7 December 2005).

[26] Professor Lynn LoPucki has argued strongly that a similar sort of management-favouring forum shopping has been rampant within the United States. L.M. LOPUCKI, COURTING FAILURE: HOW COMPETITION FOR BIG CASES IS CORRUPTING THE BANKRUPTCY COURTS 16 (2005) ("Beginning in 1990, the bankruptcy forum shopping produced an unexpected dynamic…within six years, nearly 90 percent of all large public companies filing bankruptcy in the United States filed in Delaware."). While in my view Professor LoPucki's rhetoric has gone too far, I have little doubt he is correct that a system that permits the parties great flexibility to choose the forum of an insolvency case will lead inevitably to selector-favourable legal rules, because the attraction of insolvency cases is a large economic incentive that legislators and judges are unlikely to resist, consciously or unconsciously. Attracting a really large case—say taking Enron from Texas to New York—is like getting a new Honda plant. See generally, In re Enron Corp., 274 B.R. 327 (S.D.N.Y. 2002) (deciding to maintain venue in New York, not Texas). The professional fees in Enron have approached $1 billion and the case is not finished. B. Wysocki Jr., "Rising Fees Charged in Bankruptcy Cases Elicit a Backlash", WALL ST. J., 4 August 2007, at B1; M. Pacelle, "Enron Bankruptcy is Fee Bonanza—Lawyers' Laundry and Bar Tabs Among $280 Million in Charges", WALL ST. J., 11 December 2002, at C1. Of course, certain powerful creditors may have effective control of management and may be the venue choosers, but in that case their interests and those of management will often coincide. See generally, H.T.C. Hu and J.L. Westbrook, "Abolition of the Corporate Duty to Creditors", 107 COLUM. L. REV. 1321, 1372 (2007) ("Under current bankruptcy law, the management of the debtor corporation in Chapter 11 controls the proceeding. If other parties – for example, secured creditors – control management, then they effectively control the corporation's reorganization proceeding through management.").

bankruptcy that is not governed by the laws of any jurisdiction that has a real connection to the debtor and its creditors and that has been biased in favour of the debtor.

Two related lines of cases in the United States may influence the future of denaturalized proceedings, even though the United States is not itself a "haven" jurisdiction. One line permits the filing of cases in the United States purporting to affect assets worldwide even where the United States is not the COMI of the debtor. The second line refuses recognition to proceedings that do not qualify as main or non-main under the Model Law, Chapter 15 of the United States Bankruptcy Code. The two lines of cases seem to be in some conflict.

The first line of cases includes two different types of situations. One type, typified by *In re Cenargo*,[27] presents no substantial contacts with the United States except the presence of assets within its territorial boundaries. In *Cenargo*, the debtor filed Chapter 11 in the United States just before its creditors filed in the United Kingdom, the debtor's home country. Although the judges in the two jurisdictions sorted out the matter, the United States court did claim worldwide jurisdiction on the basis of the debtor's minimum contacts with the United States.[28]

The second type of case is *In re Avianca*,[29] where the principal Colombian airline filed for a Chapter 11 reorganization in New York. The court refused dismissal sought by the aircraft lessors, arguing that the United States had a better law for the case than Columbia because the United States law would give the debtor more bargaining power with the lessors by not permitting "rejection" of the leases. Colombia's legislature had recently adopted a new insolvency law and apparently decided not to advantage debtors in the relevant respects. The United States court's ruling effectively overrode that decision. The United States case had a much stronger connection to the debtor in *Avianca* than in *Cenargo*. Nonetheless, *Avianca* was not a "main" proceeding in the sense used in the Model Law, yet the court approved a plan with global effect

The other line of cases is lead by *In re Bear Sterns*.[30] Most observers agree that these cases have established a rule that the United States will not recognize minimum-contact cases under Chapter 15. Insofar as a non-main proceeding is recognized, Chapter 15 of the United States Bankruptcy Code,

---

[27] *In re Cenargo International, PLC*, 294 B.R. 571 (Bankr. S.D.N.Y 2003).

[28] See also *In re Yukos Oil Co.*, 321 B.R. 396 (Bankr. S.D.Tex. 2005) upheld Cenargo-like technical jurisdiction, but was dismissed on the grounds of prudence rather than traditional bases like forum non conveniens or abstention.

[29] *In re Aerovias Nacionales de Colombia S.A. (In re Avianca)*, 303 B.R. 1 (Bankr. S.D.N.Y. 2003). My analysis of this case first appeared in *Economic Law and Justice in Times of Globalisation: Festschrift for Carl Baudenbacher* 777 (2007).

[30] *In re Bear Stearns High-Grade Structured Credit Strategies Master Fund, Ltd.*, 374 B.R. 122 (Bankr. S.D.N.Y. 2007), aff'd 389 B.R. 385 (S.D.N.Y. 2008) . *In re Basis Yield Alpha Fund (Master)*, 381 B.R. 37 (S.D.N.Y. 2007); *In re Tri-Continental Exchange Ltd.*, 349 B.R. 627 (Bankr. E.D. Cal. 2006).

enacting the Model Law, would permit relief only as to assets closely related to the non-main jurisdiction, rather than giving that court's rulings global effect.[31] It would seem anomalous that the United States would exercise global jurisdiction in either type of case when it would not recognize such jurisdiction exercised by other courts. However, the United States courts should take jurisdiction of either type of case where there is no other proceeding pending for the limited purpose of seizing and realizing upon United States assets for the benefit of creditors.[32]

Corporate Groups and the UNCITRAL Project

Great difficulties arise from the fact that most multinationals do business through subsidiaries incorporated, headquartered, and operating in many different jurisdictions.[33] From the largest perspective, it is not justifiable either to ignore the corporate form or to treat these entities as entirely separate.

No jurisdiction has very good answers in their own domestic laws to the host of questions created by corporate groups, and therefore it is best to focus on the specifically international aspects of the problems.[34] Solely for the purposes of international recognition and cooperation, it is possible to define a corporate group on a "one-way" basis, which describes a certain set of corporate relationships as a corporate group and identifies the parent in that group without attempting to resolve other situations that are less common or more controversial.

For example, we could define a parent corporation as one having an ownership interest when it legally controls the selection of the company's board of directors. We could use that definition to define a corporate group. We could then adopt a limited set of rules for that instance. For example, where a parent of a corporate group files in the parent's COMI jurisdiction, that jurisdiction could be the COMI for the whole group, as defined.

An approach like this would not address all instances but would act as the same sort of first-step approach as was taken with the Model Law on Cross-Border Insolvency.

II – The Future of Insolvency: Public or Private?

Introduction

Insolvency law is nearing a global crossroads in determining whether proceedings will be primarily public or primarily private. While some advocate adoption of "contractualist bankruptcy," which would permit parties to contract in advance for

---

[31] Bankruptcy Code §1521(c).

[32] J.L. Westbrook, "Multinational Insolvency: A First Analysis of Unilateral Jurisdiction", 2008 Norton Annual Review of International Insolvency.

[33] P.I. BLUMBERG, K.A. STRASSER, N.L. GEORGEAKOPOULOS AND E.J. GOUVIN, BLUMBERG ON CORPORATE GROUPS § 1.01 (2d ed. Supp. 2007).

[34] A substantial caveat to that conclusion is that UNCITRAL Working Group V is working hard on suggestions for domestic reform, as well as international cooperation: ww.uncitral.org/uncitral/en/commission/working_groups /5Insolvency.html.

The Intersection of Insolvency and Company Laws

a legal scheme managing any future general default,[35] others contend that public control is necessary both to protect important public interests implicated in a general default and to correct market failures.[36]

Legal systems around the world present these two choices. The United Kingdom and many common law countries have operated the insolvency system largely as a private one, with little or no attention to a public or third party interest. On the other hand, most civil law systems, such as the French system, have treated financial distress as implicating public and third party interests. While the rights of creditors were taken seriously in these systems, they were often subordinate to a number of other concerns.[37]

The United States system has been somewhere in between. While secured credit law in the United States has had greater scope and given more control to the secured party than in the French system, United States bankruptcy law has exerted strong control over the exercise of the secured party's rights.

---

[35] See, e.g., D.G. Baird and R.K. Rasmussen, "The End of Bankruptcy", 55 STAN. L. REV. 751, 754-55 (2002).

[36] See, e.g., E. Warren, "Bankruptcy Policymaking in an Imperfect World", 92 MICH. L. REV. 336 (1993); E. Warren and J.L. Westbrook, "Contracting Out of Bankruptcy: An Empirical Intervention", 118 HARV. L. REV. 1197 (2005); J. Sarra, Creditor Rights and the Public Interest, Restructuring Insolvent Corporations (2003).

[37] R. Blazy et al, "Financial versus Social Efficiency of Corporate Bankruptcy Law: the French Dilemma?", available at: ssrn.com/abstract=1116681 (December 2007).

The Contractualist Position

A number of scholars have argued for privatizing the insolvency laws by proposing ex ante contractual arrangements.[38] For example, Professor Robert Rasmussen proposed a "bankruptcy [insolvency] menu" consisting of a series of standard schemes for default management, where a firm picks a set of provisions it thinks best. The choice could not be changed without the agreement of all creditors, with some exceptions such as for involuntary creditors.[39]

Professor Alan Schwartz proposes an insolvency contract that will pay management to choose the right alternative, because he believes "private" benefits to those controlling the firm acts as the main obstacle to efficient default management.[40] Other scholars, such as Professor Tracht,[41] are content to leave insolvency law as it is, but want to give debtor and creditor freedom to waive the legal rules in advance.

Developments in the United States

The trend toward privatization of insolvency in the United States has three main components: the increase in dominant security interests, granted after a company has become financially distressed; broad exemptions from bankruptcy for unregulated financial institutions; and the increasing use of privately appointed insolvency trustees.

---

[38] See, e.g., R.K. Rasmussen, "Debtor's Choice: A Menu Approach to Corporate Bankruptcy", 71 TEX. L. REV. 1 (1992).

[39] For voluntary creditors, he argues as follows: "This problem is easily remedied. It is beyond peradventure that mandatory rules can be justified as protecting third parties. It is clear that non-consensual creditors need such protection. They do not, however, need the protection of a mandatory bankruptcy regime. The question of the appropriate treatment of non-consensual claimants when a firm is insolvent is the subject of a rich literature. This Article does not, and need not, enter this debate. Rather, once policymakers decide the optimal treatment of non-consensual creditors, this treatment should be unalterable by any debt contract. In other words, the priority status of tort claimants should not depend on which bankruptcy option a firm selects. Thus, a bankruptcy regime consisting primarily of default rules can readily accommodate the existence of non-consensual claimants." Id. at 66-67.

[40] This approach has been called a "bribe" to management. Note that this sort of solution is necessary, because these authors want to avoid any public official from making any important decisions in these matters, so that right conduct must be "incentivized"—that is, bought—rather than prescribed.

[41] M.E. Tracht, "Contractual Bankruptcy Waivers: Reconciling Theory, Practice, and Law", 82 CORNELL L. REV. 301 (1997). See also S.L. Schwarcz, "Rethinking Freedom of Contract: A Bankruptcy Paradigm", 77 TEX. L. REV. 515, 517-18 (1999) (explaining that scholars are debating not only whether debtors should be allowed to waive bankruptcy protections "but also whether parties should be allowed to contract for bankruptcy procedures that are different from those supplied by the state.").

The Rise of Secured Party Control of Chapter 11

Creditors have increased their control of United States reorganization cases through dominant security interests. In many cases the "bankruptcy veto" has transformed DIP control into secured party control. Because Chapter 11 may be used for liquidation and most companies file for Chapter 11 rather than Chapter 7, the secured party controls both liquidations and reorganizations.

This development differs from the traditional common law practice and from the contractualists' theories because the dominant security interest is granted after the company is in financial distress, often by larger businesses that had resisted granting broad security rights prior to their financial distress. Because the secured party will control any subsequent liquidation or reorganization, the grant of the dominant security interest is, in effect, a private bankruptcy.

So far, there is no theory supporting the economic benefit of these post-distress security interests.[42] Although post-distress priority permits financing that enables an out-of-court settlement, opaque resolution is not necessarily preferable in this age of greater financial transparency. Furthermore, one of the principal theoretical justifications for security interests is that they make default results predictable, thus lowering transaction costs. Yet post-default security interests make pre-distress credit extension by other creditors substantially riskier, because at any future time a secured creditor might obtain a priority over the pre-existing debt.

The Exemption of Financial Assets From Insolvency Proceedings

A second element of privatization in the United States has come from the recent expansion of an exemption from insolvency of certain types of financial assets, making insolvency proceedings irrelevant for quasi-financial companies whose balance sheets consist mostly of such assets. Because the moratorium of bankruptcy does not apply to these assets, the counterparties to the transactions represented by these assets may walk away with their value, leaving nothing for an insolvency administrator to administer.[43]

Privately Appointed Administrators

"Turnaround managers" and "Chief Reorganization Officers" are privately appointed, often by influential insiders, even though they perform the duties of a publicly appointed insolvency administrator.[44] It is not clear why the choice of an

---

[42] The theoretical justifications for security interests have focused on ex ante, pre-distress lowering of transaction costs and the development of long-term relationships with lenders. See J.L. Westbrook, "The Control of Wealth in Bankruptcy", 82 TEX. L. REV. 795, 841-42 (2004); R.E. Scott, "A Relational Theory of Secured Financing", 86 COLUM. L. REV. 901, 917-19 (1986).

[43] Lehman Brothers, Sharper Image, Bennigan's, and Beyond: Is Chapter 11 Working?: Hearing Before the Subcomm. On Comm. and Admin. Law of the H. Comm. on the Judiciary, 110th Cong. (2008) (statement of J.L. Westbrook, Professor, University of Texas School of Law).

[44] One duty that is arguably neglected is that of investigation of pre-insolvency wrongdoing by insiders.

administrator to take over a struggling business should be made in the dark by insiders who have their own interests at stake in the proceeding.[45]

International Developments

Because dominant security interests are the key to privatization of insolvency, the international context seems more daunting for the contractualists than the United States domestic market. So far, secured credit law remains quite parochial, although substantial efforts are underway to make some security interests enforceable internationally.[46]

The Public Interest

These moves toward privatization implicitly assume that no great public interest is at stake in insolvency cases, beyond providing a mechanism for enforcing private rights. In general, free-market societies vary greatly as to what sorts of contract and property rights will be enforced, while adhering to the overall theme of party autonomy. On the other hand, insolvency law has been an area where mandatory rules exist in every jurisdiction, reflecting public interests that are seen to transcend bargains between private parties. In the case of private contracts overriding public insolvency rules, these externalities may be divided into two categories: effects on identifiable third parties and effects on society at large.

Third-Party Effects

An insolvency affects three categories of identifiable third parties: employees and suppliers, involuntary creditors, and quasi-involuntary creditors.

Employees and Suppliers

Employees have two distinct interests in their employer's financial crisis, as creditors and as jobholders. Virtually all insolvency systems give some priority to employees as creditors whereas some insolvency systems give employees sufficient influence over the reorganization process that they may be able to protect their interests as jobholders.

---

[45] Although these appointments must be approved by the bankruptcy judge, they are presented as a change in the management of the DIP, so the tradition of DIP control in Chapter 11 leaves most courts prepared to accept any qualified person presented by the "DIP." The nominee generally being highly qualified as a technical matter, there is little consideration of the source of his or her appointment. One of the abiding theoretical weaknesses of United States bankruptcy scholarship is the failure to figure out who this DIP entity really is and under what circumstances the DIP right to control has ceased to have a rationale.

[46] A. Veneziano, "Uniform Law on Secured Transactions and Insolvency: The Approach of the Cape Town Convention and of the UNCITRAL Legislative Guide on Secured Transactions", in SHARING INTERNATIONAL COMMERCIAL LAW ACROSS NATIONAL BOUNDARIES: FESTSCHRIFT FOR ALBERT H. KRITZER 527 (2008). See www.uncitral.org/uncitral/en/commission/working_groups/6Security_Interests.html.

In many systems, suppliers are given a priority as creditors through the device of a vendor's lien, but they rarely have rights as to their interests in preserving an on-going customer.

Involuntary Creditors

The two most prominent types of involuntary creditors are tort victims and taxing authorities.

Virtually all commentators in the United States agree that tort creditors should be protected, although those committed to contractualism are more likely to believe the protection should come in some scheme outside the insolvency system with no effect on recoveries within that system.[47] However, in almost all countries tort victims have been given no special priority in insolvency.[48]

Although taxing authorities have been far more successful than tort claimants in gaining priority treatment, there has been a recent retreat from granting tax priorities.[49] Yet the public purse is an involuntary creditor that has no opportunity to bargain for its built-in extension of credit and failure to replenish the treasury has important ramifications for public policy.[50]

---

[47] Whether the notion that tort issues should be ignored in insolvency debates is sensible is a subject for another day. Suffice to say here that there are substantial objections to that notion, including the fact that the problem of fixing compensation for tort victims is fully resolved in tort law in most countries. It is precisely in the case of insolvency that the victims face the risk of non-payment, so it seems odd to think the solution to that risk lies somewhere outside the insolvency system.

[48] Professor LoPucki proposed some years ago that tort victims be given a priority over secured parties. L.M. LoPucki, "The Unsecured Creditor's Bargain", 80 VA. L. REV. 1887, 1896 (1994) (crediting B.E. Adler, D.W. Leebron, M.J. Roe, C.M.E. Painter, R. Rasmussen and P. Shupack with writing on the subject of tort creditors' priority over secured creditors.). The idea was that a secured party would be careful to ensure that the debtor maintained adequate insurance to the benefit of all concerned. Id. at 1906-1907. This idea was so sensible and fair that it has been completely ignored.

[49] *Protecting Employees and Retirees in Business Bankruptcies Act of 2007 (H.R. 3652): Hearings Before the Subcomm. on Comm. and Admin. Law of the H. Comm. on the Judiciary*, 110th Cong. 61 (2008) (testimony of B. Ceccotti) (One lawyer testified that "while it may be appealing to say 'we are giving a greater priority to employee benefit claims,' it is important to keep in mind that by doing so, you are likely to be diminishing the recovery of other types of creditors, such as taxing authorities."); M. Balz, "Equity Auctions and a New Concept of Priority: Two Bankruptcy Reform Proposals", Mar. 1, 2001, available at: papers.ssrn.com/sol3/papers.cfm? abstract_id=264511 (discussing the overall inefficiencies of granting priorities to certain creditors, including taxing authorities, as well its inconsistency with the notion of creditor equality); I.F. Fletcher, "UK Corporate Rescue: Recent Developments – Changes to Administrative Receivership, Administration, and Company Voluntary Arrangements – The Insolvency Act 2000, The White Paper 2001, and the Enterprise Act 2002", 5 Eur. Bus. Org. L. Rev. 148 (2004) ("Section 251 [of the Enterprise Act] achieves a significant reform of the treatment of company assets in insolvency by eliminating the preferential status formerly conferred on Crown debts.")

[50] E. Warren and J.L. Westbrook, "Contracting Out of Bankruptcy: An Empirical Intervention", 118 HARV. L. REV. 1197 (2005). Note that in most countries taxing authorities are granted special powers of collection under non-insolvency law.

Quasi-Involuntary Creditors

Some creditors, such as public utilities and landlords, have a relationship with the debtor that is not entirely involuntary, but is so constrained by law and circumstance that they may be considered to fall into the category quasi-involuntary.[51]

Societal Interests

There seem to be three sorts of societal interests in insolvency cases separate from the interests of identifiable parties: effects on sectors of society; social process; and the risk of systemic economic crises.

Effects on Sectors of Society

Although rarely reflected in legislation, major justifications for reorganization rather than liquidation include protection of employment and the substantial interest communities have in the stability created by long-established economic activity.[52] There are also certain sectors of private activity that have a strong direct connection to larger interests, as with financially distressed nursing homes and utilities.

Social Processes

In recent years there has been a powerful worldwide trend toward greater transparency in economic activity.[53] Transparency in insolvency matters has several benefits, including the following:

[51] E. Warren and J.L. Westbrook, "Contracting Out of Bankruptcy: An Empirical Intervention", 118 HARV. L. REV. 1197, 1216 (2005).

[52] E. Warren, "Bankruptcy Policymaking in an Imperfect World", 92 MICH. L. REV. 336 (1993); J. Sarra, supra note 36.

[53] B. Biais et al., "European Corporate Bond Markets: transparency, liquidity, efficiency", Centre for Economic Policy Research (May 2006), www.cepr.org/PRESS/TT_CorporateFULL.pdf (discusses the consequences and desirability of transparency in the European bond market.); P. Dunne et al., "European Government Bond Markets: transparency, liquidity, efficiency", Centre for Economic Policy Research (May 2006), www.abi.org.uk/BookShop/ResearchReports/TT%20GovernmentFULL.pdf (states that "transparency is a key attribute of a typical financial market."); P.M. Geraats, "ECB Credibility and Transparency", European and Financial Affairs (June 2008), ec.europa.eu/economy_finance/publiations/publication_summary12716_en.htm (argues that ECB credibility will be enhanced by embracing greater transparency about the ECB's objectives, macroeconomic forecasts and decision-making.); European Commission: European Economy, Public Finances in EMU – 2008 (2008), ec.europa.eu/economy_finance/publications/publication12832_en.pdf (transparency of budgetary projections is the ultimate goal for Member States of the European Commission.); European Commission: European Economy, Public Finances in EMU – 2007 (2007), ec.europe.eu/economy_finance/ publications/publication338_en.pdf (includes a budget transparency index and states that there has been a focus on results and budget transparency in OECD member countries.); Financial Stability Forum, "Report of the Financial Stability Forum on Enhancing Market and Institutional Resilience" (Apr. 2008), www.fsforum.org/publications/r_0804.pdf (analyzes the importance of transparency in increasing the resilience of markets and institutions.); U. Dadush and J. Nelson, "Governing Global Trade", Finance & Development (Dec. 2007),

The Intersection of Insolvency and Company Laws

- Improvement of public understanding of economic changes that often substantially disrupt the lives of people and communities;
- Reduction of corruption through institutional arrangements that provide independent scrutiny of the process;[54]
- Providing incentives for the major actors to act in socially responsible ways because of reputational concerns;
- Protection against political pressures, especially concerning necessary but unpopular economic decisions.

Systemic Crises

Financial distress may arise in two different contexts, "ordinary course" insolvency and systemic financial crisis. It may be necessary to provide distinct standards and processes for each context. Ordinary course insolvencies that come along in a stable and growing economy present a different balance of private and public interests than does a systemic crisis. In the latter case, the public interest becomes much more important, government involvement may be necessary as well as inevitable, and creditor interests may in some respects take a back seat to larger concerns.[55] Recent economic difficulties may carry forward more focus on systemic crises and the public interest in insolvency proceedings.

www.imf.org/external/pubs/ft/fandd/2007/12/dadush.htm (credits the trading system's transparency as one reason amongst others that the multilateral trade system is succeeding worldwide); D. Burton and A. Zanello, "Asia Ten Years After", *Finance & Development* (June 2007), www.imf.org/external/ pubs/ft/fandd/2007/06/burton.htm (briefly mentions that the IMF has been involved in transparency initiatives throughout Asia); A. Eftimie and M. Stanley, "Pioneering New Approaches in Support of Sustainable Development in the Extractive Sector: Background Paper on Government Tools for Sector Sustainability" (Dec. 2005), www-wds.worldbank.org/external/ default/WDSContentServer/WDSP/IB/2006/04/28/000090341_20060428104852/Rendered/PDF/359430Governm e1d0to0ESM31001PUBLIC1.pdf> (describes the Extractive Industry Transparency Initiative which requires transparency in revenues from mining companies in Africa).

[54] For example, this element is provided in the United States by the United States Trustee system. 28 U.S.C. §581(a) (Oct. 27, 1986) (Duties of United States Trustee). See COLLIER ON BANKRUPTCY, App. Pt. 4(d), at 95-98, 108-109 (A.N. Resnick and H.J. Sommer eds., 15th ed. rev. 2008) (explaining that the creation of the United States trustee "will eliminate the cronyism that exists in many parts of the country in the appointment of trustees by bankruptcy judges" and "will go far toward reducing the appearance of the bankruptcy system as run by a 'bankruptcy ring.'"). See D.A. SKEEL, JR., DEBT'S DOMINION: A HISTORY OF BANKRUPTCY LAW IN AMERICA 76 (2001).

[55] J.L. Westbrook, "Systemic Corporate Distress: A Legal Perspective", in World Bank Institute, RESOLUTION OF FINANCIAL DISTRESS (Stijn Claessens, Simeon Djankov & Ashoka Mody eds, 2001).